Invincible
Microbe

Invincible Microbe

TUBERCULOSIS

AND THE NEVER-ENDING SEARCH FOR A CURE

Jim Murphy *and* Alison Blank

CLARION BOOKS
An Imprint OF HarperCollins *Publishers*
Boston New York

www.clarionbooks.com

The Library of Congress has cataloged the hardcover edition as follows:
Murphy, Jim, 1947–
Invincible microbe : tuberculosis and the never-ending search for a cure / Jim Murphy,
Alison Blank.
p. cm.
Includes bibliographical references.
1. Tuberculosis—Juvenile literature. 2. Microorganisms—Juvenile literature. I. Blank,
Alison. II. Title.
QR201.T6M87 2012
616.9'95—dc23
2011025951

ISBN: 978-0-618-53574-3 hardcover
ISBN: 978-0-544-45594-8 paperback

Manufactured in China
LEO 10 9 8 7 6 5

———●———

This book is dedicated to

Ellen Frankovitch

and

Bob Kritcher,

whose steadfast friendship and love

have the power to heal

———— ● ————

The Lord will smite you with consumption,
and with fever, inflammation, and fiery heat, and with
drought, and with blasting, and with mildew; and
they shall pursue you until you perish.
—Deuteronomy 28:22

Yet the captain of all these men of death that came
against him to take him away was the consumption,
for 'twas that that brought him down to the grave.
— John Bunyan, *The Life and Death of Mr. Badman* (1680)

Tuberculosis—the disease which destroyed more than five
million lives last year, whose indiscriminate path through man's
recorded history has filled more graves than war, famine,
or pestilence—has been stopped.
—From the radio broadcast *Science on the March* (1953)

No matter how carefully we scour the world
for substances that kill bacteria and viruses,
eventually we are going to lose the battle.
—Robert Baker, *Quiet Killers: The Fall and Rise of Deadly Diseases* (2008)

———— ● ————

CONTENTS

A 1917 poster shows the Grim Reaper looming large over a crowded and dirty street in France. The text reads: "A Great Scourge—Tuberculosis."

THIS IS THE STORY

THIS is the story of a small, harmless-looking germ that has been infecting people for millions of years.

It's the story of how this microorganism became the greatest killer of humans in the history of the world; of the terrified, desperate people invaded by this tiny creature, and what their families and friends tried to do to save their lives; of artists who painted pictures and authors who wrote adoring stories about these doomed sufferers; of how physicians struggled for centuries to find a cure for their illness; and of a miraculous medical discovery that finally stopped the killer of billions of humans—only to have this germ stubbornly evolve again into something even more insidious and deadly.

This is the story of tuberculosis.

Homo erectus *was the first of our prehistoric ancestors to journey outside of Africa, carrying TB.*

One
IN THE BEGINNING

F IVE hundred thousand years ago a small band of our ancient human ancestors, now known as *Homo erectus,* traveled across western Turkey. One of them, a young male, had been sick for many weeks. He was tired and irritable, and his head ached terribly. For days he hadn't been able to eat much, and what he did eat, he soon vomited up. Still, he tried to keep up with the rest of his group. But as they entered a mountain forest, the pain in his head became unbearable and he could no longer walk.

There wasn't much anyone could do for him. They brought him water and tried to make him comfortable. No matter what they did, the pain in the boy's head continued until he was so sick, he no longer recognized his companions. Finally, moaning in pain, he lay on the ground and fell into a deep sleep from which he never woke.

His people never knew what killed him. But modern-day scientists do. When paleontologists studied a fragment of this boy's fossilized skull, they saw a series of tiny lesions, or scars, on the inside. The scars were identical to those made by a bacterium that causes a fatal disease of the brain. What the scientists were looking at was the oldest physical evidence of tuberculosis (TB) yet discovered.

The origins of TB actually go back even further than this. Scientists now believe that TB is caused by microorganisms that lurked in the soil and water of Africa as much as 3 million years ago. By chance, some of our most ancient ancestors became infected with these TB germs and died from the disease. Later, between 20,000 and 35,000 years ago, something happened: The germs began to evolve. What emerged was a different and even more dangerous microorganism, which we call *Mycobacterium tuberculosis*.

my ko back TEE ree um too bur kew LO sis

M. tuberculosis is a slender, elegantly curved rod, so small that 25,000 of them laid end to end would measure only one inch long.

View of the inside of the fossilized skull of a young male Homo erectus. *The stylus is pointing to the tiny lesions made by a form of tuberculosis that infects the brain.*

A scanning electron micrograph image of Mycobacterium tuberculosis.

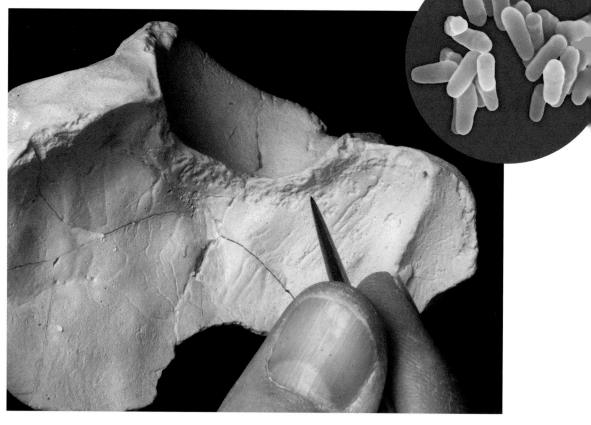

They grow much more slowly than other bacteria and are bound up in a fatty, waxlike protective wrapping. When observed through a microscope, they look more harmless and beautiful than deadly.

Yet *M. tuberculosis* is anything but harmless, mainly because these germs can be passed so easily from person to person. When individuals with these microorganisms in their lungs cough, sneeze, or simply talk, they spew millions of bacteria into the air in tiny droplets. These seemingly innocent germs can then hang in the air for several hours, until someone else breathes them in.

Once inside a human body, the *M. tuberculosis* bacterium usually finds a comfortable home in the lungs. But these germs have the remarkable ability to establish themselves in other parts of the body as well. They can survive in and infect the large and small intestines, the lymph nodes, the skin, bones, and joints, the brain,

A single sneeze sends millions of tiny droplets into the air.

the eyes, the inner ear. . . . In fact, there is almost no organ or tissue in the human body that is immune to this germ.

Once situated, the TB germ begins to multiply. Over the course of days, hundreds of thousands and then millions of them will appear and begin to eat into the organ, bone, or tissue. In the case of tuberculosis of the spine, this process can take many years, during which time the back bones collapse and a painful hunchback develops. Sometimes the advance of TB is much less predictable. A person with *M. tuberculosis* in his or her lungs might die in a few days or weeks. Or the illness might linger for months, even years. It can also disappear suddenly, only to return years later. Even today, scientists have no idea why TB is so unpredictable, but they do know that whenever TB of the lungs is active (that is, when the bacteria are multiplying), each cough can send millions upon millions of *M. tuberculosis* into the air to infect anyone who comes near.

As various groups of *Homo erectus* and then their modern human descendants, *Homo sapiens,* left Africa and wandered around the world, tuberculosis germs accompanied them. Then 15,000 years ago another change took place that further encouraged the spread of the disease. Modern humans began to farm and raise animals such as cows, horses, chickens, and dogs.

Certainly the advent of farming and herding produced many positive results. With ready access to food, people were less likely to starve, and human populations began to grow. However, the increase in population also had some far less desirable results. Isolated agricultural settlements began to grow into villages, towns, and thriving cities. The living quarters in these permanent settlements tended to be small, cramped, and lacking in ventilation. Such cavelike conditions were ideal for the spread of infectious diseases, such as malaria, cholera, typhoid, diphtheria, and, of course, TB.

Adding to the problem was a second form of TB: *Mycobacterium bovis.* This germ looks almost exactly like *M. tuberculosis* and has also existed for millions of years. It can infect a wide variety of animals, including deer, foxes, and badgers, but it is most commonly found in herds of cattle. As *M. tuberculosis* had done, *M. bovis* evolved until it could infect humans. People's increasing reliance on cattle raised for their meat and milk meant that TB had a second way to come into contact with and invade the human body.

These two forms of TB infected people for thousands of years. One member of a family might be struck down while the others were spared, but sometimes entire families became ill and died. And whenever people carrying the TB germ traveled—to marketplaces, to religious ceremonies, to neighbors' homes, and to nearby towns—they spread TB to many of those they encountered.

A crowded medieval market scene.

my ko back TEE ree um   BO vis

The existence of numerous ancient Egyptian paintings portraying hunchbacks with spinal tuberculosis proves that it was a common ailment 5,000 years ago. And the disease wasn't confined to the poor. The mummified body of the high priest Nesparehan, who died some 3,000 years ago, has the large hunchback of someone who suffered from spinal TB.

An ocean away in Peru, testing of a 2,700-year-old mummy indicated that the ten-year-old boy suffered from TB of the lungs, liver, kidneys, heart, and spine. In fact, studies of hundreds of other skeletal remains and mummies in India, China, and North and South America have revealed that the disease existed in these regions well over 1,000 years ago.

By then there were few places on earth where humans could go to escape the disease. And while tuberculosis had been stalking and infecting our ancestors for hundreds of thousands of years, there was very little anyone could do for those who contracted it. Of course, people tried. Sometimes soothing teas were brewed from plants, tree bark, or herbs. Sometimes a poultice—a gooey paste of ground-up, moist substances—would be mixed, heated, and applied directly to the area of the body that hurt. In some places shamans or medicine men used magic rituals and prayers, hoping a god or gods would help with a cure.

The first system of healing developed in Egypt's Nile Valley. Egyptians began formally practicing medicine over 6,000 years ago, and they passed their accumulated medical knowledge from one generation to the next in schools called Houses of Life. Often priests from the temples would also train to be doctors.

Egyptian medical knowledge was written down on

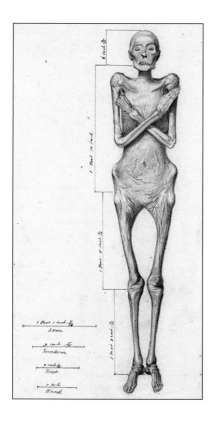

A drawing from 1825 by Dr. Augustus Granville of a mummified woman who died of tuberculosis.

A page from the Ebers Papyrus. The text discusses "a painful finger or toe . . . their odor being malignant, whereas they have formed maggots." The physician is advised to bandage the injury with a poultice made from honey, ochre clay, cannabis, hedjou resin, and ibou plant.

scrolls of papyrus, a thick paperlike material made from the papyrus plant. A number of these scrolls still survive, with one, known as the Ebers Papyrus, close to sixty-six feet long. On it are discussions of numerous internal and external ailments, along with 877 recipes for poultices, teas, and 400 different drugs.

The medical advice in these papyruses tended to be straightforward and sensible in response to a visible condition, such as a head wound. But because microorganisms are invisible to the naked eye, the physicians didn't know that germs existed and caused diseases. As a result, Egyptian doctors often looked to other causes to explain as well as cure these more mysterious ailments. A disease like TB of the lungs, for instance, was thought to be the work of angry gods or the result of an enemy's spell. Prayers were said to expel the evil, and patients wore amulets to protect themselves from further invasion.

Once the evil had been driven out, the physician would treat the physical ailment. In the case of TB of the lungs, patients might be told to gargle with a concoction of mashed garlic and equal parts of water and vinegar to lessen their coughing fits.

Physicians in ancient Egypt understood the limits of their healing powers. When a physician encountered an illness he knew he could cure, he would confidently tell the patient it was "an ailment I will treat." If he wasn't sure he could cure it, he would say it was "an ailment with which I will contend." But when a person with TB began coughing up dark-red blood, the physician would say it was "an ailment not to be treated," pronouncing the patient's death sentence.

Sadly, little progress was made in understanding TB for several thousand years. The disease spread and caused thousands upon thousands of people to die painful deaths while friends and physicians watched helplessly.

One small advance was made about 1000 B.C., when Greek physicians first recognized TB damage to the lungs as a specific disease and documented its symptoms. They described how people with the disease grew pale and emaciated, developed noxious-smelling night sweats, were often short of breath, and coughed up blood as they grew sicker. One Greek professor of medicine, Sylvius, associated the tiny nodules always found in diseased lungs with the illness and called them tubercles, from which the word *tuberculosis* was derived. The Greeks also gave the disease that damaged lungs

THIGH sis

its first medical name, phthisis. This Greek word means "a dwindling or wasting away."

For hundreds of years Greek doctors observed and described phthisis in great detail and worried that it was spreading unchecked. In 460 B.C. the famous Greek physician Hippocrates called phthisis the most dangerous epidemic of his time. He noted sadly that it was infecting an unusually high number of children and was "almost always fatal."

The Greeks had a comprehensive way to explain health and

A print made by the Italian artist Cintio d'Amato in 1671 shows a physician opening a patient's vein while an apprentice catches the blood in a small basin.

Two physicians preparing the cure-all medicine theriac from a secret recipe that could include more than sixty ingredients.

illness that did not involve evil spirits. They believed that the human body contained four key fluids, called humors: blood, yellow bile, phlegm, and black bile. As long as the humors were in balance, the individual would remain healthy. If one or another of the humors built up or diminished, illness would soon follow. The Greek physician's job was to help patients get their humors back in balance.

Correcting the balance could be accomplished by something as simple as a good diet, bed rest, and drinking a soothing tea. With more serious illnesses, the excess humors might be expelled from the patient's body by giving the sick person drugs to induce diarrhea or vomiting. But with a lingering illness like tuberculosis of the lungs, truly drastic steps were needed. When a patient coughed up blood, for instance, the physician would diagnose an excess of blood. To put the humors back in balance, he might slice open a vein to allow some of the patient's blood to drain away, a procedure called bloodletting. The more blood an individual coughed up, the more blood a doctor would take from him or her, often until the patient fainted.

The Greeks may have also treated TB with a concoction called theriac, which was originally formulated to combat snake bites. Theriac contained between twenty and sixty-four different ingredients (including alcohol and opium) and took months to mix and ferment. It eventually was seen as a cure-all for many illnesses, including TB, though it did little more than relieve the sick person's pain.

Many of these extreme attempts to cure TB did absolutely no good, and actually may have harmed patients by weakening them physically. But since there were no other options, people who could afford a doctor's services still sought out medical help.

TB continued to march forward unchecked through the centuries, infecting an ever-widening number of people. And because there was no effective way to treat and cure the disease, those who developed the persistent cough of phthisis knew they were doomed. But that all changed shortly after A.D. 1000, when word of a miraculous and painless new cure spread throughout Europe.

Two
THE KING'S EVIL

FOR days in the spring of 1490, people had gathered at the royal palace in London. Blacksmiths, candle makers, tavern keepers, house servants, nuns, rope makers, soldiers and sailors, farmers and their families—hundreds of them crowded into the courtyard awaiting the arrival of King Henry VII of England.

While their backgrounds and occupations varied, all these people had one thing in common: a disease known as the king's evil. It was scrofula, a disease caused by *M. tuberculosis* when it infected the tiny, bean-shaped lymph glands in the neck. Scrofula was generally painless, but it produced a bluish-purple lumpy mass in the person's neck. Sometimes the mass would grow so large that it would rupture, causing an open wound. Those suffering the king's evil had come with the hope that Henry would cure them by simply touching the infected area.

According to some legends, the practice of the "royal touch" was begun by King Edward the Confessor. He was a pious man who ruled England from 1042 until his death in 1066. Once the king touched the bulging mass of a sufferer, he usually allowed

SKROF you la

the patient to stay at the royal palace until cured. The majority of those who stayed were incredibly poor and malnourished. It is now believed that the regular diet and rest they received at the palace may well have succeeded in making them physically stronger, even if it didn't cure them of scrofula.

After King Edward was gone, English kings and queens who succeeded him also claimed to have "the royal touch." The power

Charles II touches patients to cure them of tuberculosis of the lymph nodes in an illustration from 1654.

to cure disease was said to have been handed down from Jesus Christ to his apostles and from the apostles only to legitimate royalty. Because of this supposed direct line to Christ, many rulers insisted that their ability to heal was a sign that their rule was divinely ordained. And since doctors hadn't yet found a cure for any form of tuberculosis, desperate people were more than willing to become believers.

By the time Henry VII came to power in 1485, a healing ceremony would draw hundreds and hundreds of sick citizens to the palace. To impress them, Henry developed a particularly elaborate ceremony that could take hours to complete. First he would enter the courtyard where the people were assembled, accompanied by long lines of his ministers, priests, court administrators, and any of the noblemen and -women who might be staying at the palace. Armed guards would maintain order while a secretary kept an accurate count of how many citizens were touched.

Next, one at a time, the sick would approach their king and kneel at his feet. A long prayer was said, and then Henry would pass his hands over the patient's sores while the chaplain asked that "God . . . grant that these sick persons on whom the King lays his hands may recover." This ritual would be repeated over and over again until every single person had been touched.

The angel or touchpiece that England's James I presented to "cured" patients between 1603 and 1625.

So many flocked to such ceremonies that there simply wasn't enough room in the palace for all of them. Additionally, it was proving extremely expensive to feed and care for them. Instead of taking them in, Henry presented each patient with a specially minted gold coin called an angel. The angel, all were told, would ward off the disease in the future.

Of course, the king's touch couldn't really cure the disease; nor could the gold coin. But the fact that the king had had contact with these people made them celebrities in their towns and villages. Friends and neighbors would buy them meals or tankards of ale, hoping they would be allowed to touch the magic coin. The improved diets of these TB sufferers often resulted in them actually feeling better for a short time.

Despite the many obvious failures of the royal touch, the practice was extremely popular in England for more than 600 years. It finally ended in England in 1702, when Queen Anne took the throne and banned the ceremony. But the healing touch was still practiced by almost every other European monarch for many diseases in addition to scrofula.

France's Philip Augustus (who ruled from 1180 to 1223) is credited with more touches in a single day than anyone else—1,500. The lifetime record for touches is held by Charles II of England (who ruled from 1660 to 1685). During his twenty-five-year reign he is said to have touched 92,102 of his subjects, which works out to 3,684 per year. The practice seems to have finally come to an end in Europe in 1886, when Austria-Hungary's emperor Franz Josef I touched and allegedly cured the son of one of his coachmen.

While tens of thousands received the royal touch every year, there were millions of sick people who couldn't attend the ceremonies. These people had to rely on relatives or a local professional healer for their care. While such healers often had no medical training, most were caring individuals trying their best to comfort and heal the sick. Others were nothing more than quacks, happy to try out bizarre "cures" for money. It wasn't unusual for unscrupulous healers to have patients swallow strange and disturbing concoctions made up of such things as ground-up human or animal eyeballs, sautéed human livers, pieces of raw snake, and even animal or human urine.

While superstition ruled the treatment of all diseases, including all forms of tuberculosis, a few dedicated physicians were trying to document and treat TB in a logical manner. In the early 1500s the Swiss-born physician known as Paracelsus wrote a detailed account of phthisis in miners from Cornwall.

Two Italian physicians were astonishingly accurate in their speculation about tuberculosis of the lungs. Girolamo Fracastoro (1483–1553) was convinced that phthisis was transmitted by invisible particles that he called *seminaria* (Latin for "seeds"). He claimed the *seminaria* could survive outside the human body and still infect.

One hundred years after Fracastoro, a professor of anatomy, Giovanni Battista Morgagni (1682–1771), also suggested that the disease was contagious. Morgagni was so concerned about this that he flatly refused to perform autopsies on victims of tuberculosis. Instead he had assistants cut open the bodies while he directed the action from a specially built viewing gallery a safe distance away. Fracastoro and Morgagni were unable to prove their theories through scientific experiments, and their ideas were largely ignored for several hundred years.

A portrait of Paracelsus by Quentin Metsys, 1550.

One reason physicians knew so little about TB three hundred years ago was that most of the medical instruments doctors rely on today, such as X-rays and stethoscopes, had not yet been invented. To gather information about a disease, a physician could only observe the patient carefully, put his ear to the patient's chest to listen to his heartbeat and lung action, and feel the person's forehead to see if he had a fever.

One of the first real steps forward in the fight against tuberculosis came in 1715, when Hermann Boerhaave from the Netherlands invented a fifteen-inch-long thermometer. It allowed him to accurately chart the rise and fall of the body temperature of ill patients. When the temperature went up, he discovered, it was a sign that the patient's TB was active and spreading.

Over a hundred years later, a French physician named René Théophile Hyacinthe Laennec created another valuable medical instrument. As part of a routine medical examination in 1818, he tried to listen to an obese patient's heartbeat but couldn't hear much through the patient's layers of fat.

Laennec thought over the situation for a few moments, and then inspiration struck. He rolled up a piece of paper, brought the paper tube to "the cardiac region and . . . was surprised [when he put his ear to the end of the tube] to hear the heartbeat much more clearly and distinctly." After a series of painstaking experiments, he fashioned a foot-long hollow wooden tube with a funnel at one end. Called a stethoscope (the Greek word *stethos* means "chest" or "breast"), this invention allowed doctors for the first time to clearly

Despite having his stethoscope in his left hand, Laennec still used the tried-and-true method of listening to a patient's lungs by putting an ear to the person's chest.

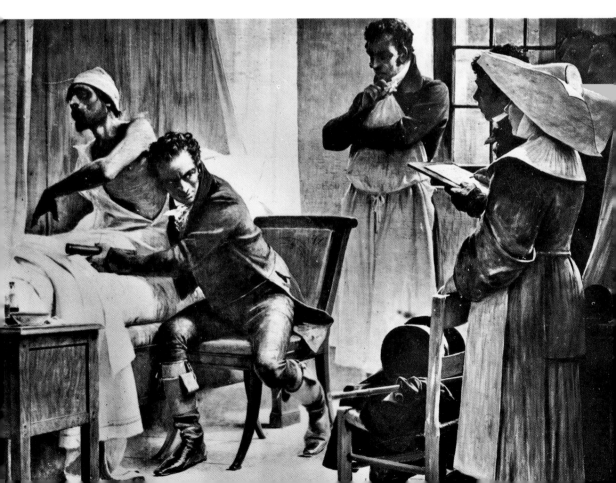

hear TB-infested lungs struggling to draw in oxygen. Ironically, Laennec's nephew diagnosed TB in Laennec using one of his stethoscopes.

As helpful as these inventions were, they did not solve the mystery of tuberculosis. No one knew what caused it; no one knew how it was spread; and most important, no one knew how to cure it. The disease was so baffling that even thoughtful and talented physicians used extreme measures in their search for a cure.

One such doctor was Jean-Baptiste Denis, who lived in France in the mid-seventeenth century. Desperate for a way to treat TB, he resurrected a 1,500-year-old theory called vitalism. This was based on the idea that the blood of a living creature, whether man or beast, somehow carried the essence of that creature (its good and bad physical and emotional qualities). According to vitalism, a bull's blood, for example, carried the animal's traits of great power and energy.

Denis then tried to take blood from a bull and put it into a human, hoping the animal's positive qualities would be passed on to his sick patient. The first few attempts to do this failed miserably, with most patients suffering terrible seizures. This didn't stop Denis, who remained convinced that his procedure could work. Then one day, for no explainable reason, a patient dying of tuberculosis not only received the blood without having a seizure but was soon healthy enough to return to work.

Denis wasted little time in proclaiming his "cure" for TB. Soon doctors throughout Europe were using animal blood to treat not only TB but every other ailment imaginable. Sadly, the hope generated by this "cure" quickly evaporated. Several weeks after his miraculous recovery, Denis's patient collapsed while at work and died. In the months ahead, every other physician who attempted the procedure reported the same fatal results.

It seemed that nothing physicians tried could halt the spread of tuberculosis, especially TB of the lungs. More and more people were heard coughing and choking for breath, their bodies slowly shriveling away as if being consumed from within. The Greek medical name phthisis would be used by doctors well into the nineteenth century, but most people replaced it with a more popular and descriptive term: consumption. By the end of the

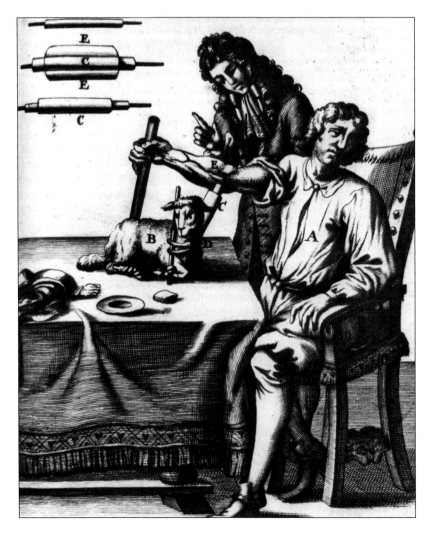

A woodcut of Jean-Baptiste Denis transfusing the blood of a lamb into the arm of a deranged patient. He hoped the lamb's gentle nature would be passed on to the man.

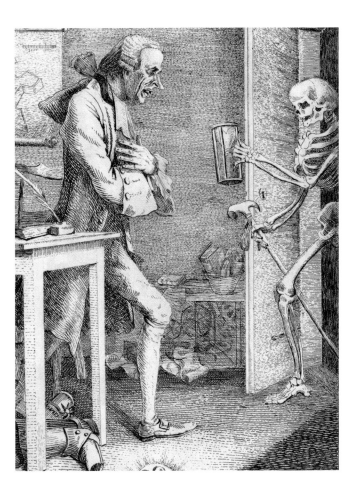

Irish-born author Laurence Sterne suffered for many years from tuberculosis. This drawing shows death finally coming for him in 1768.

eighteenth century the toll taken by consumption was growing each year at an alarming rate. More than a century earlier one writer, John Bunyan, had called it "the captain of all these men of death." His description was still appropriate, and while no one knew it, things were only going to get worse.

Three

"THERE IS A DREAD DISEASE"

IT was a hissing, clanking metal monster that caused TB's next deadly surge among humans. James Watt's 1765 improvements to a very primitive steam engine made that engine faster, safer, and more fuel efficient. The improved engine launched the Industrial Revolution. Within a few years businessmen and engineers from around the world were using Watt's steam engines to power the machines in their factories.

Over the following decades a global mass migration of people took place as millions abandoned farmwork and rural living to operate steam-powered machines in factories. By the mid-nineteenth century, cities such as London, Paris, Madrid, New York, and Boston all underwent explosive growth. Cities everywhere expanded their borders and swallowed up neighboring towns and farms. Between 1800 and 1850 the population of New York City grew from 60,000 to over 500,000.

For all but the very rich, housing in cities had always been cramped and unsanitary. Now the rush to build homes and structures to house the new workers made conditions even more

An 1898 photograph of crowded Hester Street on New York's Lower East Side.

hazardous and deplorable. In Dublin in 1850, for instance, almost 40 percent of the housing stock consisted of only one room, and 98 percent of these rooms housed at least five people.

These were the ideal conditions for the spread of a droplet-borne infection like tuberculosis. And spread it did. One modern microbiologist has estimated that by 1850 between 75 to 90 percent of *all people on earth* had the TB germ in them, and that 20 percent of these people developed active cases of the disease. "Tuberculosis," Dr. Thomas L. Dormandy noted sadly, "slaughtered the poor by the millions."

Many children worked twelve-hour days in cramped, dangerous factories. After work, they went to crowded, filthy dormitories to sleep, often two to a bed. An 1840 report by England's Children's Employment Commission stated that a startling number of seven- and eight-year-olds were "stunted in growth, their aspect pale, delicate, sickly, presenting a race which has suffered from gross physical deterioration." What caused this? The commission concluded that it was "disease of the lungs ending in atrophy, consumption and death."

Overcrowded cities also saw an alarming increase in crime, which meant bigger prisons were needed. These were soon packed wall to wall with prisoners, often eight to ten convicts to each small, windowless cell. This, too, was a perfect breeding ground for TB. Half of all prisoners in England's Chatham Naval Prison died of TB every year between 1870 and 1880. In the United States before

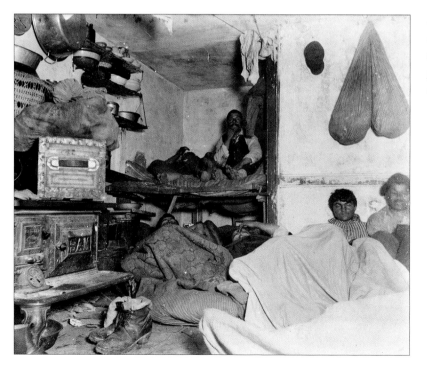

A Jacob Riis photograph entitled Five Cents a Spot *shows a group of very poor men crammed into a single room.*

1910, no one serving a life term in any prison survived longer than twelve years.

Even those outside the sickly confines of the city couldn't completely escape the grasp of tuberculosis. Living a communal life where everyone worked and ate together, thousands of monks and nuns around the world grew sick and died. The creator of the stethoscope, Dr. Laennec, oversaw one French nunnery from 1809 to 1819. During this period he observed, "After being one or two months in the establishment, [the young sisters] became suppressed . . . and phthisis declared itself. . . . I witnessed [the death of entire groups of nuns] two or three times owing to the successive loss of all its members."

Whether young or old, good or bad, a consumptive on the slow road to death was a miserable, lonely sufferer. His or her last days were plagued by constant coughing to expel fluid from the lungs, foul-smelling night sweats, and frequent bouts of diarrhea and vomiting. Attempting to put their humors back in balance, doctors and their helpers usually caused patients even more pain. Even if the doctor didn't use extreme measures to cure a patient, the person's final hours were spent slowly choking to death on his or her own bodily fluids.

Death by TB was awful. But, surprisingly, the images of the tuberculosis patient that made their way into newspapers, magazines, and books and onto the stage were altogether romantic in nature. Many people—including those with tuberculosis—thought the thin, emaciated body and pale, almost translucent skin of a consumptive were beautiful. Henri Amiel, a Swiss philosopher who had TB, wrote in his journal, "Decay and disease are often beautiful like the hectic glow of consumption." So popular was the consumptive look during the nineteenth century that some fashionable young women drank a concoction of lemon juice and vinegar or ate sand, hoping to destroy their appetite and make themselves look pale and alluring.

In addition, having consumption was frequently associated with being creative. The notion was that the disease gave the sufferer stronger emotions and a clearer and more profound sense of the world around him or her. The French writer Alexandre Dumas noted sarcastically, "It was the fashion to suffer from the lungs; everybody was consumptive, poets especially."

The list of artists who were consumptives is remarkably long and includes the poets Friedrich von Schiller, John Keats, and Percy Bysshe Shelley; the writers Edgar Allan Poe and Robert Louis Stevenson; the composers Franz Schubert, Frederic Chopin, and Niccolo Paganini; the artist Aubrey Beardsley; and one of America's first African American poets, Paul Laurence Dunbar.

Probably the best-known consumptives of the nineteenth century were the Brontë sisters Charlotte and Emily. Their mother died from consumption at age thirty-seven while they and their three other sisters and their brother were still young. Their father did what he could to keep his family together, but several years later the four oldest girls, Maria, Elizabeth, Charlotte, and Emily, were sent away to a boarding school.

It was a ghastly place, always cold and dank, where the children slept in crowded rooms. A few months after the Brontë girls' arrival, an unidentified epidemic swept through the school, sickening forty girls, including Elizabeth and Maria. The sisters became so ill with a painful and persistent cough that they were sent home. Just a few months later, both died from consumption. They were only eleven and ten years old.

The remaining Brontë children went on with their lives in apparent good health. Charlotte, Emily, and Anne wrote stories and managed to get their first pieces of fiction published. But

Anne, Emily, and Charlotte, the three remaining Brontë sisters, as painted in 1834 by their brother, Branwell, who also died of the disease.

eventually the tuberculosis lurking inside them flared up. In 1835 Emily grew pale and weak and developed a cough that lingered. Soon after, Anne developed a similar cough and found it difficult to breathe.

In 1848 their brother, Branwell, developed the severe chest pains and hacking cough of an ever-worsening case of consumption. He died a short time later. Three months after his death, twenty-nine-year-old Emily also died. A year later, advanced consumption took Anne as well.

The lone surviving sibling, Charlotte, lived for another six years, seeing both her novel *Jane Eyre* and her sister Emily's posthumously published *Wuthering Heights* become international bestsellers. She married in 1854, and soon became pregnant. At around the same time, she fell seriously ill with symptoms suggesting to her doctors that she had consumption, though recently some scholars have questioned this diagnosis. This last Brontë child died a year later at the age of thirty-nine.

The Brontë sisters and other consumptive artists often wrote about the disease and their experiences with it. Several characters in *Wuthering Heights* die of consumption. Writers who did not have tuberculosis also included frequent references to TB or characters with the disease in their works. For most of the nineteenth century such characters appeared in novels, poems, and operas, usually dying in a remarkably dignified, spiritual, and generally painless way. As Edmond and Jules de Goncourt put it in their novel *Renée Mauperin,* "Phthisis is an illness of the lofty and noble parts; it calls forth a state of elevation, tenderness and love, a new urge to see the good, the beautiful and the ideal in everything, a state of sublimity which seems almost not to be of this earth."

Even when someone spoke the harsh truth about TB—that those who had it would inevitably die in a painfully horrible way—the statement always seemed to contain a note of brightness. "There is a dread disease," wrote Charles Dickens in his novel *Nicholas Nickleby,* "which so prepares its victims . . . for death. . . . A dread disease in which the struggle between the soul and body is so gradual, quiet and solemn, and the result so sure, that day by day and grain by grain the mortal part wastes and withers away, so that the spirit grows light and sanguine with its lightening load."

Doctors had to deal with the sad reality of the disease and the fact that for all of their experience with TB, there was still no cure. Most physicians continued to balance a patient's humors, though some were happy to try out gentler folk remedies and exotic new medicines. Others prescribed trips to warmer, drier climates such as the American West, the Pacific islands, and countries in the Middle East, hoping the sun and dry air would clear the lungs of mucus.

The vast majority of people around the world had to find ways to deal with TB as best as they could. In northern Europe and the United States, it was commonly believed that certain people were born with a predisposition for the disease. And since so many

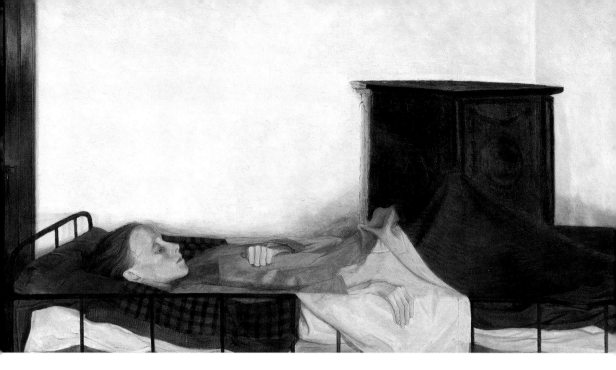

people living in poorer sections of cities got TB, the obvious conclusion was that their poverty in some way made them predisposed to contract TB.

In nineteenth-century Italy and other southern European countries, on the other hand, people came to believe the disease was contagious, even though there was no scientific proof at this time. Travelers suspected of having consumption were routinely turned away by hotel owners and their possessions burned. Both those who believed the disease was hereditary and those convinced that it was contagious were trying to accomplish the same thing. By blaming others for the epidemic, they were able to assure themselves that they and their families were to some degree safe. It was a frail and foolish façade.

Then in the mid-1850s a twenty-seven-year-old medical student came up with a method of treatment for consumption that would still be used a century later. Oddly enough, it was based on nothing more than a bit of medical mumbo jumbo.

Four
INTO THE MOUNTAINS

H ERMANN Brehmer was studying medicine in Berlin in 1853 when a twenty-year-old theory about the cause of tuberculosis came to his attention. Several German and Austrian doctors had suggested that consumption was caused by a weak heart. The blood of a TB patient, they believed, wasn't being pumped through the body with enough force to flush out the disease.

None of these doctors bothered to test this theory in a scientific manner. And neither did Brehmer. Instead, in his doctoral paper, Brehmer simply proclaimed the theory to be absolutely true. He backed up the claim by stating that he'd observed many weak hearts in postmortem examinations of victims of consumption (though in truth he'd participated in very few autopsies).

He then invented a course of treatment. Consumption was curable in its early stages, he boldly stated—again, without any scientific backing. His answer was largely scientific double talk: Get the patient quickly into the pure air of the mountains, he directed, where "the reduced atmospheric pressure [at higher elevations] would ease the pumping action of the heart muscle." This, in turn,

Hermann Brehmer created his sanatorium cure based on very little scientific research.

would improve the overall condition of the body and help it fight off the disease. He supported his theory by quoting world-famous explorer Alexander von Humboldt, who claimed that TB did not exist in any of the world's mountainous countries. This was absolutely untrue.

Brehmer was so taken by his own theory that the following year he established the first institution specifically designed to treat tuberculosis of the lungs. He called this medical facility for long-term illness a sanatorium (from the Latin word *sanatorius,* which means "health giving"). In fact, when his TB sanatorium opened in the Bavarian mountain village of Görbersdorf, it was little more than several hastily nailed-together shacks. But Brehmer's steadfast promise of a cure made Görbersdorf an instant success.

There was more to Brehmer's treatment than simply hanging around in the fresh mountain air to improve the flow of blood. He rejected the traditional, often harsh, methods of treatment, such as bloodletting and the use of drugs to cause vomiting and diarrhea. Instead, he intended to help patients strengthen themselves physically from head to toe so that the body could ward off TB. To accomplish this, he proposed a regimen of carefully supervised walks through the forest, bed rest, and a nutritious diet. He or one of his assistants would always be present to monitor the patients.

None of Brehmer's ideas was particularly new. The notion that the body was its own best healer was the foundation of the ancient Greek theory of humors. Brehmer was, however, a great self-promoter. Not only did Görbersdorf continue to expand over the years, but other tuberculosis sanatoriums began springing up throughout Europe.

One of the most famous was founded in Germany by a cured ex-patient of Brehmer, Dr. Peter Dettweiler. Dettweiler made what he considered several improvements on Brehmer's cure, but his real

Brehmer built his sanatorium in Görbersdorf into the very large institution pictured here in the 1870s.

claim to fame was something quite simple. He was the first doctor to keep detailed records of his treatment of each patient's illness and publish these findings in important medical journals. Over a ten-year period, he wrote, he'd treated 1,022 victims of consumption and been able to cure 542 of them. While modern physicians dispute his cure claim as wildly exaggerated, it was an impressive-sounding success rate. It captured the attention and imagination of doctors and sufferers of consumption around the world.

Many other sanatoriums also claimed a degree of success that rivaled the Brehmer/Dettweiler treatments, often adding their own unique twists to the original regimen. Dr. Otto Walther created a special diet to strengthen his patients' bodies that required them to eat massive amounts of milk, cheese, meat, potatoes, butter, fruit, and sweets every day. Whether it worked or not will never be known, because Walther never allowed his records to be published. But his patients seemed to love the diet. One consumptive from England reported happily, "It is amazing the amount one can eat when forced to."

(Top) A class of tuberculosis sufferers raking hay in Dr. Rollier's Sun School in Switzerland.

(Bottom) An early-twentieth-century panoramic view of children with tuberculosis on the front lawn of a TB sanatorium in Liverpool, England.

Some sanatoriums used soothing music to keep patients calm and relaxed, while others tried to forbid excess mental stimulation (such as the reading of books). They believed that a tired brain was just as dangerous as a tired body. What was common among all these emerging institutions was that a patient's life was carefully and, in some cases, severely regulated. Patients weren't allowed to leave the sanatorium without permission, and they woke up, ate, took their temperature, exercised, and went to sleep under strict supervision.

While popular in Europe, the idea of sanatoriums didn't catch on in the United States for some time. The credit for its eventually happening rests entirely on the frail but determined shoulders of a consumptive doctor named Dr. Edward Livingston Trudeau.

In the spring of 1873 Trudeau believed he was dying. As a teenager he had nursed his older brother, who had died from TB. He'd also come in contact with the disease while treating it in his medical practice in crowded New York City. Now, suffering from advanced TB, Trudeau decided to retreat to the wilderness of the Adirondack Mountains, not to seek a cure but to spend his last remaining days in a place he loved.

At the time, the Adirondacks was a vast area of untouched forests in upstate New York, "visited," Trudeau recalled, "only by hunters and fishermen." While the Adirondack landscape was beautiful, with its many lakes and rugged mountains, "it was looked upon as a rough, inaccessible region" with a "most inclement and trying climate" that included fiercely cold and snowy winters. Trudeau's out-of-the-way destination was forty miles from the nearest train station, and the wagon trip over rocky, rutted roads so exhausted him that he had to be carried into the sportsmen's hotel where he was staying.

In the weeks to follow, Trudeau spent his days being rowed across pristine mountain lakes, strolling along forest paths, and napping under towering pines. Remarkably, his fever disappeared, then his night sweats vanished. By the end of the summer, instead of wasting away and dying in his beloved mountains, Trudeau had gained fifteen pounds and was completely cough-free. When his return to New York City quickly brought back his symptoms, Trudeau, along with his wife and their young child, moved permanently to the town of Saranac Lake.

The idea of setting up a sanatorium of his own came to Trudeau in 1882 after he read about the Brehmer/Dettweiler cure regimens. They sounded remarkably like his own daily routine in the mountains, so Trudeau decided to test the theory out on some of his own patients. Trudeau's innovation was to establish a sanatorium so that "poor, sick people in cities could . . . have the chance of improvement I had had by coming to the Adirondacks."

Two years later, he opened the Adirondack Cottage Sanatorium and received its first two patients. At the time the sanatorium consisted of one tiny red cottage fourteen feet wide by eighteen feet long with "a little porch so small that only one patient could sit out at a time, and with difficulty."

When Dr. Edward Trudeau arrived in the Adirondack Mountains, he was so weak, he could barely stand up. But in a photo taken after three months of fresh air, good food, and exercise, he appears remarkably healthy.

A replica of "Little Red," the first cure cottage at Trudeau's Saranac Lake sanatorium.

From this humble beginning, Trudeau's sanatorium would grow bigger and more influential every year. Eventually, the Adirondack Cottage Sanatorium would have fifty-eight buildings on a rolling landscape of eighty-five acres. The single one-room cottage would give way to larger cottages that accommodated a number of patients at the same time. In addition to the patient cottages, the campus would include a large administrative building, an infirmary for bedridden patients, a training school for nurses, a research laboratory, a chapel, and even its own post office.

The village of Saranac Lake also changed. While many other towns and cities shunned TB patients, the inhabitants of Saranac Lake embraced them as if they were long-lost friends. The people of Saranac Lake didn't seem to fear TB, perhaps because the idea that tuberculosis was a contagious disease was not universally accepted. Additionally, because locals firmly believed that their climate was unusually healthy, they may have thought it would protect them from the disease. After all, what could they possibly fear if the very air they breathed was the cure?

Whatever the reason, local adults eagerly signed up to help care for the waves of arriving patients, while children brought the sanatorium guests magazines and ran their errands for a few pennies. Requests for admission to Trudeau's sanatorium far outnumbered the available beds, and local residents gladly picked up the slack. They began building houses that included open-air porches where sick individuals could sleep or sit in the sun year round. In time, the hunting- and fishing-guide business that had sustained the village for decades was replaced by what came to be called the curing industry.

The success of Trudeau's sanatorium prompted demands for similar institutions in other areas of the country. From that single red cottage in the New York wilderness, the American tubercu-

losis sanatorium system eventually grew to number 536 facilities taking care of more than 673,000 men, women, and children at a time.

A patient poses with her husband and children in front of a private cure cottage in Saranac Lake, New York.

These institutions created a unique lifestyle that many patients hated, some tolerated, a few even enjoyed, and all endured because it offered something no hospital could—the hope of a cure.

Five

"TO COMFORT ALWAYS"

IN 1937, writer Betty MacDonald learned she had TB of the lungs and would have to go to a sanatorium, and she panicked. "Sanatorium, I knew what that meant," she would later write in her book *The Plague and I*. "Sanatoriums were places . . . where people went to die."

The knowledge that you had a disease with no known cure must have been extraordinarily frightening. It would be comparable to being told you had AIDS or late-stage cancer. And while going to a sanatorium offered a ray of hope, it came at a steep emotional price. You had to leave family, friends, and home—everything that was familiar—and face an unknown future alone. As author and TB patient Robert Louis Stevenson wrote about his horse-and-buggy ride to Saranac Lake:

> *Crack goes the whip, and off we go;*
> *The trees and houses smaller grow;*
> *Last, round the woody turn we swing;*
> *Good-bye, good-bye to everything!*

The way patients were greeted when they arrived at the sanatorium was critical to how quickly they felt comfortable in their new surroundings. Dr. Trudeau was known for his warm and optimistic spirit and went out of his way to welcome every new patient. His well-known credo—"To cure sometimes, to relieve often, to comfort always"—fostered a positive attitude among staff members and the surrounding community that helped put nervous newcomers at ease.

Not every sanatorium was so friendly. The one Betty MacDonald went to in Oregon was "a depressing place filled with golden oak benches, stale air and other people with tb." Instead of a friendly greeting, the nurse at the sign-in desk had a "tight-lipped, unsmiling, unfriendly attitude [that] was a shock to me. . . . Apparently she hated people with tuberculosis the way some people hate liver."

In most sanatoriums, patients had to adjust to a rigid and

Exercise was part of the Trudeau cure. Here Dr. Trudeau (center) glides across a frozen pond with two of his patients. The one on the right is believed to be Robert Louis Stevenson.

unvarying daily schedule and a long list of rules. They would be awakened at six thirty A.M. to have their temperature taken, drink hot milk, and bathe themselves with what one patient recalled was a very "cold sponge." This would be followed by breakfast, then two hours outdoors in a chair or bed, even in the winter, and then a period for doing crafts. Hour by hour, sometimes minute by minute, the rest of the day proceeded in much the same regimented fashion. Lights-out and bedtime came early, usually by nine P.M., and if possible, patients slept outdoors on unheated porches, even in the dead of winter.

When Trudeau's sanatorium first opened, he tried to keep rules

Patients curing at the Adirondack Cottage Sanatorium after a snowstorm.

to a minimum. But as the years passed, a list of do's and don'ts developed. One patient remembered that as soon as he arrived at Trudeau's sanatorium, a nurse appeared "with a rule book, which I was supposed to read and sign. It had my number on it—8027. I felt worse than ever. Like I was in prison."

Some institutions were extremely aggressive about making rules, following the advice Dr. Paul Kretzschmar gave in an 1888 article. "The smallest details of the patient's life," Kretzschmar wrote, must be "controlled by the supervising physician and nothing of any importance should be left to the patient's unsupported judgment." Such details included what could and could not be placed on the nightstand, which books could be read, when talk was permitted, the type of music a patient could listen to, and even who was to turn lights on and off. Betty MacDonald remembered asking why certain personal items were being taken from her. Instead of a logical answer, the nurse snapped out a list of rules: "Patients must not read. Patients must not write. Patients must not talk. Patients must not laugh. Patients must not sing."

In such places, there was no easing into the sanatorium regime. After being signed in, patients were immediately ordered to bed and not allowed to get up for anywhere from a week to several months. The goal was to have patients completely abandon their former routines and get used to the sanatorium lifestyle as quickly as possible.

"Pretty nearly all TB patients regard their doctors as enemies at first," journalist Marian Spitzer wrote about her own experience in the 1930s, "and most of the doctors know it." Many patients rebelled at losing their active lives and their freedom, though how they resisted varied from individual to individual. Some talked back to staff members or refused to follow the prescribed regimen. Others protested in more modest ways, such as secretly reading a

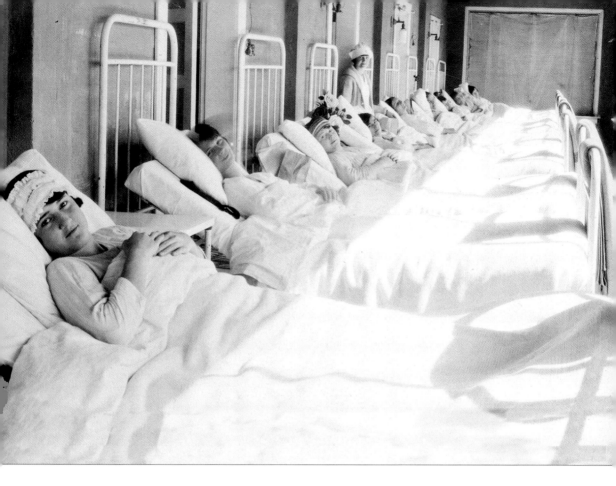

Girls taking the cure on a porch at the State Tuberculosis Sanatorium in Texas.

forbidden book or talking when talking was not allowed. Betty MacDonald relied on her sharp wit to help the days pass. After being chided by the night nurse for a minor offense, MacDonald laughed to herself and thought, "There's one thing to be said in favor of life at The Pines. It's going to make dying seem like a lot of fun."

Of course, no one at a sanatorium wanted to die. They had asked to be admitted and had agreed to the terms of confinement specifically to cure the disease that was slowly eating away their bodies. But they did have to come to terms with the new reality of their lives. In MacDonald's case, a nurse eventually set her straight. "We are going to make you well," the nurse barked, "and the shortest distance between two points is a straight line. Here is the line, either follow it or get out."

In the end, it was in the patient's interest to lose this emotional struggle for control and follow the sanatorium's regimen—mainly because it did prolong life. While few patients actually left a sanatorium fully cured, a substantial number did have the advance of their TB checked and were able to return to their former lives.

How can this be explained? Doing away with bloodletting and the use of harsh drugs meant that the patient's body was not assaulted and weakened unnecessarily. Further, the focus on strengthening the patient with rest, a good diet, and gentle exercise allowed the body to fight, and sometimes stop, the spread of the disease. Finally, many doctors, including Trudeau, speculated that being outdoors somehow strengthened the lungs.

Handicrafts, such as pottery and leatherworking, were a common recreation at many sanatoriums.

Trudeau set up an experiment to see how living conditions could affect health. He took fifteen rabbits and divided them into three groups of five. He placed the first group of healthy rabbits in a damp, dark pit with only a little food and water. He infected the second group with TB and housed these rabbits in a crowded box in a cellar. Those in the third group were also given TB, but they were released on an extremely small island on St. Regis Lake near the sanatorium. The island offered the rabbits plenty of food, water, and sunshine.

After several months, Trudeau examined his test subjects. In the first group, the uninfected rabbits were all alive but clearly malnourished. Those in the second group of rabbits, with TB, were all dead. It was the infected rabbits in the third group that proved

An older and frailer-looking Trudeau working in his laboratory in 1895.

most surprising. One rabbit had died of the disease. The rest not only were alive and active but had no signs whatever of TB.

To Trudeau, the fact that most of the rabbits released on what came to be known as Rabbit Island survived proved that sunshine and decent food could arrest the advance of TB. In fact, modern-day bacteriologists have acknowledged that there is some truth to Trudeau's conclusion. They note that being outdoors so much allowed a TB patient to absorb a great deal of vitamin D from the sun. Vitamin D produces a molecule called *cathelicidin,* which is known to attack and kill tuberculosis bacteria.

kath a LISS a din

The youngest sanatorium patients often had the hardest time adjusting to the required changes. Some institutions built special facilities for patients under the age of sixteen, such as the Child's Infirmary at Trudeau's sanatorium. In other places, children might be segregated in a wing of the main building or mixed in with the general population.

No matter how an institution tried to accommodate them, children must have felt a profound sense of dislocation and anger. "I was 16," Marie Shepitka recalled of her journey to the Trudeau sanatorium, "ill with a disease that required a long stay in a sanatorium 300 miles from home, taken from a world that was just beginning and tossed helplessly on a heap of despair."

Eighteen-year-old Marie Shay spent an entire day traveling by train to Saranac Lake "in tears, crying constantly" and arrived after the sun had gone down. The place where she was to stay was fairly large and housed two dozen other patients. "The cottage may have been normal enough in daylight," she remembered, "but it appeared an ominous hulk in the dusk, a very dismal drab grey or green, not the sort of house a fresh-faced teenager would choose to die in."

Plunged into the cure routine, young patients were ordered to rest in bed, ordered to get up at a certain hour, ordered to keep track of their weight and temperature, ordered to eat everything served to them. The orders were endless. And when a young patient protested, he or she was told to follow the order or risk dying. The result was that some went about the day in a gloomy funk. Marie Shepitka was confined to bed with a view of the distant mountains. She was, she recalled, "a shy, scared, sick teen-ager, noticing no

These children are in class in Pittsburgh's first open-air school, which was located on the rooftop of a settlement house.

beauty in the surrounding countryside, smothered in the fear of uncertainty and aloneness."

As the days passed and young patients got used to the routine, they often found ways to make themselves feel more in control of their lives. Marie Shay recalled, "We were told to put nothing on the walls [of our rooms] and to keep our dressers uncluttered. I put up all kinds of banners and pennants on my walls and pictures of my family everywhere on the dresser. I wanted my room to look like home." Fifty-nine years after her stay in Saranac Lake, Shay gleefully concluded her story with "And I got away with it."

Mabel Sharp was just sixteen when she was sent to the New York State TB sanatorium at Ray Brook. After spending nine months essentially confined to "cure chairs on unheated porches," she decided she needed a change. She transferred to the Trudeau sanatorium, where, in addition to curing, she entered the D. Ogden Mills School of Nursing and became a registered nurse.

A young boy with TB shows off his "Eskimo suit"—a two-piece pajama suit with a hood, made of heavy wool blanket.

Eventually, the vast majority of patients young and old came to accept their new lifestyle, and many even came to look back on their days in a sanatorium with genuine fondness. Although Marie Shepitka began her stay "on a heap of despair," when she finally left, she had to admit, "If only I had known then that something so seemingly devastating would be the start of a new world for me. . . . Those four years . . . molded my character and are in many ways responsible for the person I am today." Marie was not alone. For some patients, friendships and romances flourished. Classes in pottery and metalworking taught them new and interesting skills. In Saranac Lake, patients wrote and published small books with messages of "good cheer" and waited with excitement for the Winter Carnival that took over the village each year. Tucked away in mountain retreats and other peaceful settings,

Children from the "Health Gun Float" at the Winter Carnival wearing signs designating various diseases. In the background, a man with the health gun is about to "cure" the illnesses.

many patients actually grew to love the fact that the outside world was a distant thought.

But as they were taking the cure, the work of a German doctor was about to transform the world of medicine—and with it the sanatorium cure—forever.

Six

THE CAUSE

ROBERT Koch began his search for the cause of tuberculosis in Germany in 1881, just one year before Trudeau read about the Brehmer/Dettweiler sanatoriums. Koch was short, nearsighted, frail in appearance, and, at age thirty-eight, already world famous. He was known for developing a way to stain bacteria with colored dyes for examination under a microscope, as well as for finding ways to culture, or grow, bacteria in a small, round dish with a cover. He had also successfully identified the specific microbe that caused the deadly disease anthrax and proved that a single anthrax germ could grow into a large, lethal colony. Guessing that the same would be true for TB, Koch began his hunt for the world's greatest mass killer.

He started by taking blood samples from a laborer who had died from miliary TB, a particularly deadly strain of the disease that invades a wide variety of body parts in a matter of days by way of the bloodstream. Koch assumed the TB would be present in the man's blood. He then injected this material into a number of guinea pigs and rabbits and observed what happened. All the animals, he wrote, "became emaciated rapidly, and died after four to six weeks." Finally, samples were taken from the animals for study; Koch reported, "Under the microscope all . . . animal tissue [samples] . . . appear faintly brown . . . with the [rod-shaped] bacilli, however, [stained] beautifully blue." He suspected that he was looking at the creature that caused tuberculosis.

Next, Koch set out to prove this. He put some of the blue-dyed bacteria in a culture dish and set them aside to reproduce. After enough had grown, he planned to inject the substance into healthy guinea pigs and rabbits. If they developed TB, he would know for certain that the blue rods were the cause of the disease.

Koch soon learned something else about *M. tuberculosis*. It was incredibly slow to reproduce itself. Most bacteria can double in number every fifteen to twenty minutes, creating a colony large

Robert Koch was so famous that a drawing of him appeared on a card included with the purchase of chocolate.

CHOCOLAT GUÉRIN-BOUTRON

KOCH

KOCH, médecin Allemand, né en 1843, découvre, en étudiant le choléra aux Indes, le bacille qui porte son nom, puis le bacille de la tuberculose, qui fait prévoir la guérison de cette maladie.

LES BIENFAITEURS DE L'HUMANITÉ

84 Sujets variés

enough to be visible in the culture dish within hours. However, it takes *M. tuberculosis* between fifteen and twenty-four hours simply to reproduce *once.* The result was that even after two weeks, nothing had appeared in Koch's culture dish.

Fortunately, Koch was as patient as he was obsessed. He continued to wait and watch until, several weeks later, a colony of *M. tuberculosis* began to appear. When he had enough, he injected the bacteria into healthy animals. Every single one developed TB. To be absolutely certain his results were correct, Koch repeated the time-consuming experiment over and over again.

More than a year later, in March 1882, Koch was able to announce his findings to an astonished Berlin Physiological Society. After describing his research, he concluded his talk by saying, "In the future, the fight against this terrible plague of mankind will deal no longer with an undetermined *something* but with a tangible parasite."

In addition to revealing the cause of TB, Koch's discovery produced two other pieces of information. First, he was able to say with certainty how the disease was spread. The germs, he announced, were "expectorated by consumptives and scattered everywhere." Second, he was able to show that the TB bacillus caused a variety of illnesses in other parts of the body besides the lungs.

Although Koch had already unmasked the anthrax germ (and had had his research verified by other scientists around the world), his new discovery was largely ignored. Most people—including many doctors—simply refused to believe that such a tiny organism could actually cause disease and kill humans. The American Medical Association completely ignored the discovery at its annual meeting later that year. And the *New York Times* failed to report the news for over a month. When Koch's discovery was finally mentioned in an editorial, the newspaper mocked Koch and the

After his sixteen-year-old sister, Sophie, died of tuberculosis, artist Edvard Munch created many paintings and etchings in her memory.

entire idea that germs were a natural part of our lives by making up a story about a fictional doctor from Wisconsin. This doctor, the editorial claimed, was such an ardent believer in the new germ theory that he had announced the discovery of a microorganism that could be "bred into trousers [so that] men will be fully protected against broken legs."

Fortunately, a few people did take notice. One of them was a New York medical student named Hermann Biggs. Biggs was a twenty-three-year-old graduate student at the time, studying pathology, a field of medical science that looks at the causes and development of diseases. He immediately saw the importance of Koch's discovery. His senior thesis on sanitary science argued that because dangerous germs were everywhere and could be spread easily, the well-being of a nation depended on the "careful observance of hygienic laws." In other words, health issues should be as vital a part of our system of laws as, say, international trade, national defense, or economic stability.

Mustering support for this position would be an uphill battle for Biggs, who became professor of pathology at New York's Bellevue Hospital in 1885. Most doctors had been trained in, and based their practice of medicine on, a belief in the humors of the body. They saw no reason to abandon a theory that was thousands of years old, and seemed to work, in favor of a new theory that had not yet been tested worldwide.

Others feared that the new germ theory would diminish their role as physicians. Until then it had been the doctor's job to

New York medical officer Hermann Biggs as he appeared in 1910.

pronounce whether or not a patient had tuberculosis. But now a diagnosis could be made only if *M. tuberculosis* was found in matter such as the patient's sputum, mucus and phlegm mixed with saliva and ejected from the mouth. Most doctors weren't capable of doing these diagnostic tests themselves.

Finally, many doctors were hesitant to embrace Koch's findings because they were legitimately worried about their patients. If it was true that the TB germ could be transmitted in airborne droplets, then the logical way to stop the disease from spreading would be to quarantine sick patients. The patients would be isolated in sterile wards with other sick and dying people and away from the love and help of their families.

Despite such resistance, the notion that steps needed to be taken to combat tuberculosis finally took hold in the late nineteenth and early twentieth centuries. Many cities and towns already had some health laws on the books. These dealt mostly with disposing of decaying dead animals and vegetable matter, because the resulting foul smells were thought to cause diseases. There were also quarantine laws to keep sick persons with certain fast-spreading diseases, such as diphtheria and cholera, separate from the healthy population.

In 1887 Scotland became the first country to institute a national antituberculosis campaign. Several other European nations followed with regulations of their own. The United States was slow to enact such laws, but that would all change with the help of Hermann Biggs.

When the now thirty-year-old Biggs joined the New York City Health Department in 1888, there were no public health laws to stop the spread of tuberculosis. A year later, Biggs was able to get a modest three-pronged program made into law. The plan called for the inspection of cows for the bovine form of TB, in order to eliminate infected meat and milk. It also required that the personal effects of a tuberculosis patient be burned and any room he or she lived in be disinfected. Finally, the city was required to begin a publicity campaign to educate citizens about TB, specifically on how it was spread and how to avoid becoming infected. Within days this information was printed in leaflets in numerous languages and distributed throughout the poorer areas of the city where the largest numbers of TB infections occurred.

Though pleased to have these laws enacted, Biggs wasn't finished. One important recommendation had been turned down, although it sounded very logical. Quite simply, Biggs wanted to require doctors to report the names and addresses of all patients with TB.

When it was first proposed, this step set off loud protests from doctors concerned about their patients' privacy. They knew that most insurance companies denied payment of benefits for anyone who died of tuberculosis. What was to stop these companies, doctors wondered, from combing through the public records to root out the unfortunate victims of the disease?

Fearing that worried citizens would vote them out of office, state politicians joined the doctors in opposing Biggs. Reluctantly, Biggs backed off slightly. Instead of ordering doctors to turn over names and addresses, he requested that they do this voluntarily for the good of the city. Few doctors handed over names, and deaths from tuberculosis in New York City stayed at approximately 6,000 per year into the twentieth century.

Biggs hadn't given up, though—not by a long shot. He knew that New York City had more than 300,000 tiny, unventilated rooms and apartments, each occupied by six to eight people packed together. Every day these places produced more and more cases of TB. "With every breath," wrote Ernest Poole of the Charity

Organization Society after inspecting several crowded buildings, "I felt the heavy, foul odor from poverty, ignorance, filth, disease."

Biggs believed passionately that altering unsanitary living conditions and using modern scientific methods would in time result in the defeat of TB. So instead of giving in to the concerns of doctors and politicians, Biggs declared war on the disease.

He turned to the newspapers and fed them a steady stream of information about the dangers of TB and how it was spread. He not only wanted to raise awareness of TB, he also wanted to create a sense of alarm in the minds of the public. It took several years, but by 1905 people came to view tuberculosis as an urgent, life-threatening health crisis. Fearful individuals began to report neighbors and relatives who they suspected had TB. And politicians became more willing to pass tougher health laws.

A nurse, medical bag in hand, climbs over New York City rooftops to visit those who are sick.

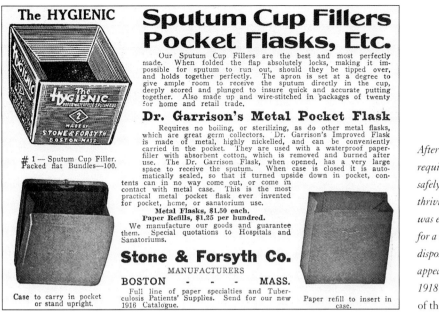

After laws were passed that required TB patients to safely dispose of spittle, a thriving spit-cup industry was established. This ad for a metal flask with disposable paper inserts appeared in the May 1918 issue of the Journal of the Outdoor Life.

In fact, the campaign worked so well that Biggs's New York Health Department was given ever-increasing powers to fight the disease. In addition to requiring physicians to report the names and addresses of TB patients, the Health Department was allowed to send nurses into homes to see if any individual had TB. His department was also authorized to have the sickest patients isolated and treated in specially established hospitals. Spitting, a habit embraced at that time by even the most refined people, came under attack. Antispitting laws were enacted, and people with tuberculosis were required to carry and use spit cups with them at all times to capture the potentially lethal sputum.

Biggs also pushed for the use of modern technology. In November 1895 a Bavarian professor of physics, Wilhelm Conrad von Röntgen, had been conducting a routine experiment of passing high-voltage electricity through a glass tube. In the darkened laboratory he'd noticed an unusual light and soon discovered that this

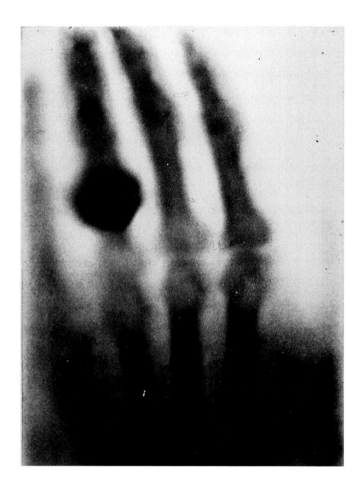

This X-ray from 1895 is the first X-ray ever made. It shows the hand of Röntgen's wife, Anna. The bump on the second finger from the left is her wedding ring.

light could penetrate solid objects. When he held his hand over it, he could see the bones inside. The use of what Röntgen called X-rays for medical purposes was slow to catch on, but eventually X-ray machines were developed that made images of the inside of the human body. Biggs saw the usefulness of X-rays in diagnosing TB and immediately ordered the newfangled machine.

The influence of Biggs and his Health Department was soon being felt in a wide variety of nonmedical areas. Because the shabby housing arrangements of the poor were considered hives of infection, a campaign was launched to develop inexpensive but healthy alternatives. The movement was spearheaded by well-known reformers, such as Jacob Riis and Lillian Ward, with Biggs behind the scenes making recommendations for new legislation. New York City's Tenement House Law was passed in 1901, specifying the number of inhabitants allowed to live together in a space. The law also provided specific minimum requirements for the size of rooms and the amount of light and ventilation they needed to have.

(Top) A young girl has a chest X-ray taken at Detroit's Herman Kiefer Hospital for Communicable Diseases in 1939.

(Below) A doctor and a nurse examine an X-ray of a patient with tuberculosis.

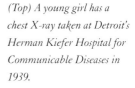

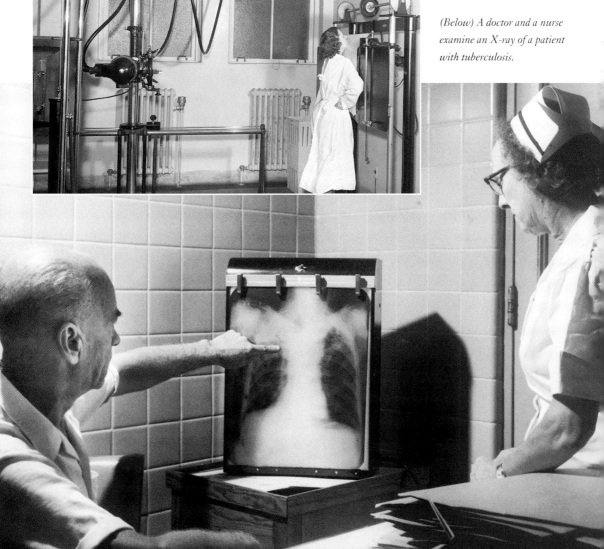

A poster for an early anti-spitting, -coughing, and -sneezing campaign.

Eventually, New York State followed New York City's lead, setting up a state sanatorium and passing a series of strict health laws. While the new policies were often criticized as cruel and unconstitutional by some doctors and politicians, they seemed to have a positive effect. By 1913 Biggs was able to boast that New York City had reduced TB deaths by 50 percent per year, thus saving an estimated 65,000 lives since the campaign had begun.

Other states noticed the gains being made with Biggs's policies and began copying New York's approach. Even European countries sent representatives to, in Biggs's words, "look to New York for suggestions and directions in new methods in sanitary work."

The local and state antituberculosis campaigns were reinforced by a national organization in 1904. Composed of prominent physicians and influential citizens, the National Association for the Study and Prevention of Tuberculosis sponsored serious scientific studies of the disease, then published and promoted the findings. This organization worked hand in hand with state and local groups in an effort to educate the public and sponsor antituberculosis laws and programs.

One of its most successful programs was the annual sale of Christmas Seals to raise money for the organization. Interestingly enough, the idea was thought up by a Danish postal clerk. In 1904 Einar Holboell, a forty-four-year-old postal worker in Copenhagen, heard that young people were dying of TB because they had no money to go to a sanatorium. He wanted to donate money but knew his small salary meant he couldn't give very much at any one time. He wondered if a surcharge of a few cents could be added to certain postage stamps, with this money going to fight TB. If enough people chose to buy those stamps, a sizable amount of money could be raised.

In less than a year the program was in place in Denmark and

14th Annual Seal Sale To Fight Tuberculosis

Legendary baseball slugger Babe Ruth helps to sell Christmas Seals in 1921.

very successful. In 1907, Emily Bissell tested out the idea in Delaware. She designed and printed special holiday seals that would be sold at the post office for a penny each and put on envelopes along with the regular postage stamp. Her first campaign managed to raise over $3,000. Her success led the national tuberculosis association to issue Christmas stamps or seals in 1908. By 1919 proceeds in America amounted to over $19 million per year. All that money went toward the fight against TB.

The world, it seemed, had at long last joined in a coordinated attack against its biggest killer. The war against TB was so successful that it created a major problem. The already crowded sanatoriums found themselves deluged with requests for treatment by tens of thousands of people. Many TB sufferers were given beds, but millions of others were left uncared for and untreated. These victims of the disease came to be called outsiders.

Seven
THE OUTSIDERS

IN November 1906 a young boy from Pennsylvania named Robert Freeman wrote an impassioned three-page letter to Dr. Lawrence F. Flick. Freeman explained that he was "a Poor boy Afflicted With the . . . Lung trouble" and that his father had "spent most all of his Money for Doctors Bill and Medicine and he [was] not able to do any thing more for [him]." He ended by begging Dr. Flick, "Take me at your Sanatorium."

Dr. Flick was the perfect person for this boy to approach. Flick had survived TB as a poor young man and had spent most of his medical career treating fellow sufferers. He'd also helped to establish several TB sanatoriums, had founded the first organization in the United States to further TB research, and was a strong advocate for the treatment of poor TB sufferers. If anyone could help Freeman, it was Dr. Flick.

Then Flick read the last line of Freeman's letter: "P.S. I am a Colored boy. Do you take Colored People?"

This was a reasonable question at a time when, sadly, the answer to such an inquiry was usually no. As outrageous as it might seem

Lawrence F. Flick led the fight against tuberculosis in Pennsylvania.

to us today, the poor and minorities were routinely denied desperately needed treatment by the very people sworn to care for them—doctors, public health care officials, and medical organizations.

When the twentieth century began, almost all private sanatoriums refused to treat African Americans, Native Americans, Hispanics, Asians, and the poor. Most public sanatoriums followed the same exclusionary policies. In Pennsylvania, for instance, only twelve of the twenty-nine public tuberculosis institutions accepted poor or minority patients, and all but a few of the twelve made it a practice to segregate African Americans and other minority patients from whites.

Flick found the situation abhorrent and actively fought against such discrimination. As a founder of Pennsylvania's White Haven Sanatorium in 1901, he made sure that the facility was open to everyone, regardless of race or religion. So letter writer Robert Freeman was extremely lucky and was admitted to White Haven.

Elsewhere, the poor and members of minority groups were literally outsiders when it came to adequate medical care. Many white doctors refused to treat them, and druggists often wouldn't sell them medicine (or, when they did, sometimes raised their prices). Some groups, however, found ways to counter such prejudice. When Irish and Italian immigrants discovered that prejudice against them continued even after they had achieved impressive financial gains, they set up their own medical schools and health facilities. African Americans did this too, and by 1870 had established seven colleges to train their own doctors and related health-care workers, such as nurses and pharmacists. And then the American Medical Association (AMA) stepped in.

The AMA was founded in 1847 by 250 white male doctors drawn from forty medical societies and twenty-eight medical col-

The poet Paul Laurence Dunbar was among the thousands of "outsiders" who had difficulty finding proper medical care and eventually died of TB. He was a teenager at the time of the poetry reading advertised in this flyer.

leges. The physicians' goal was to meld these various groups into one powerful national organization to "promote the science and art of medicine and the betterment of public health."

From the beginning the AMA refused to allow African Americans and other minorities to join their organization or any of the regional branches that sprouted up in the following years. This decision profoundly limited the number of nonwhite doctors practicing medicine in the United States. After medical school, training to be a doctor required two years of work (called a residency) in a hospital. And in order to be a resident in a hospital, an individual had to be a member of a recognized medical society.

In 1879, after several failed attempts to gain admittance to the AMA, African American physicians created their own fully integrated organization, the National Medical Society (NMS). When NMS members still found themselves barred from most hospitals, the group asked repeatedly to be admitted to the AMA. These requests were always denied. In 1900, the U.S. Bureau of the Census counted 132,002 physicians in the United States. Of these, a mere 2,200 were African American. This number represented only 1.7 percent of the physician population, although at the time African Americans actually accounted for nearly 12 percent of the U.S. population.

Still, seven medical schools were training African Americans to be physicians, so the number of African American physicians slowly increased over the years. And then the AMA struck again. In 1908 it launched a study of all medical schools in the United States, allegedly to standardize and raise their level of education. The study was headed by noted educator Abraham Flexner, who visited all 155 medical schools in the United States before issuing his report.

Many schools were very good, he concluded, but "there is probably no other country in the world [where] there is so great a distance and so fatal a distance between the best . . . and the worst." His conclusion was that the AMA should give more financial support to the good institutions and work for "the speedy demise of all others."

Over the following years, nearly half of all medical schools in the United States were denied state and federal funding and were forced to shut their doors or were merged with other institutions. Of the seven schools where African Americans studied to be doctors, five were closed. The Flexner Report, the AMA today admits, "caused a disproportionate reduction in the number of physicians servicing disadvantaged communities . . . [leaving] impoverished areas with far too few physicians."

Despite the prejudice of the AMA and the majority of white doctors and hospitals, there were some advances in the treatment of the poor and minorities with TB. In Pennsylvania the state legislature passed bills in 1907 to combat TB in the poor, voting to build one or more additional sanatoriums, plus smaller facilities called dispensaries, each of which was associated with a hospital

Tuberculosis was predominantly a disease of the poor. This mother, father, and child all have TB.

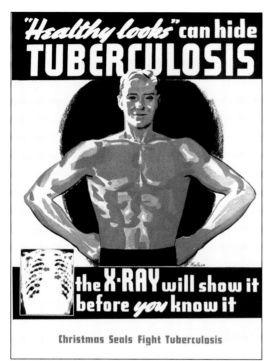

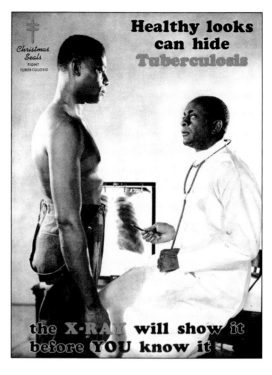

Two 1930s ads from the Christmas Seals campaign, warning, "Healthy looks can hide tuberculosis." The one featuring an African American doctor and patient was displayed only in areas with large African American populations.

and drew on the hospital's medical staff for support. By 1910 Pennsylvania had in operation 115 dispensaries for poor TB patients. This was a promising beginning—but only a beginning. Sadly, the demand for beds far exceeded the number of beds available.

From the late nineteenth century to well into the twentieth, massive numbers of African Americans left the southern United States to resettle in the north. Nearly two million African Americans headed to northern cities between 1915 and 1930, a population shift that has come to be called the Great Migration. In Philadelphia the migration resulted in a 58.9 percent increase in the African American population between 1910 and 1920 and a 63.5 percent increase by 1930.

Most of these people migrated to escape the oppressive conditions of a prejudiced South and to find work in factories and shops in the industrial north. Many thousands also hoped to find proper medical care for chronic conditions such as TB. In Pennsylvania the sanatorium and dispensary health-care system that could accommodate several thousand patients suddenly found itself deluged with tens of thousands of TB sufferers. While African Americans worked to establish their own local tuberculosis associations, hospitals, and sanatoriums in cities like Detroit and in states like Virginia and South Carolina, their valiant efforts could only address the needs of a modest few.

Whether white or African American, those turned away had few options. Trying to replicate sanatorium conditions, many built crudely constructed "cure porches" on the roofs of their apartment

People who were unable to enter a sanatorium often built their own shelters at home. Here a woman sits in her tent on the roof of her New York apartment building.

buildings or in the small, dark lots behind them. The majority suffered miserably in their tiny rooms with only the help of caring family and friends. Many thousands simply had to leave their hometowns to seek medical help.

A good number of these people "chased the cure" west to states that offered fresh air and a dry, warm climate. A major destination of TB sufferers was southern California. During the latter part of the nineteenth century, many communities there actively tried to lure what was known as the "invalid trade" to their towns. In one promotion article that appeared in *Land of Sunshine* magazine, the author declared, "A consumptive who can live in sunshine year in and year out has chances for life not obtainable under other conditions." Meanwhile, in a nationally distributed travel brochure, the head of the San Bernardino, California, Immigration Association called the area "Nature's Great Sanatorium."

Nellie Crosby, shown here with her baby on the dirt floor of her home, was denied professional treatment for her tuberculosis because she was Native American.

The campaign proved highly successful, and each arriving train brought more and more TB sufferers to southern California. This boom in population—and the subsequent economic gains—was widely applauded, and other warm-weather western states, such as Arizona and New Mexico, copied the campaign. Then came Robert Koch's 1882 discovery of the TB bacillus and of the fact that the disease was highly contagious.

The first response in these magnet areas was a mixture of surprise and panic: How could we have been so foolish as to let tens of thousands of contagious individuals into our state? This was followed by: Now what do we do?

In California the answer to the second question came from the head of the California Board of Health, John L. Pomeroy, and the head of that board's Bureau of Tuberculosis, Edythe Tate-Thompson. Both Pomeroy and Tate-Thompson were strong-willed, determined leaders who quickly came to a firm decision. Improved treatment for tuberculosis was vital, but, they argued, it should only be available for "us" (California citizens) and not "them" (poor immigrants from other states and nations).

The state Board of Health was charged with preserving the health of California citizens, which Pomeroy generally interpreted to mean its white citizens. Thus, African Americans who traveled to and became legal residents of California faced the same discrimination and shortage of medical care as they had elsewhere in the United States. Of the fourteen TB hospitals and sanatoriums in and around Los Angeles in 1923, only two admitted African Americans. There was also very limited space available to African Americans in nursing and medical schools. Those who were admitted faced continuous prejudice and humiliation.

African Americans weren't the only ones targeted for discrimination. Legal and illegal immigrants from Mexico, Japan, and the

Philippines were also on Pomeroy's list of problems. He began by demanding that the federal government seal the border between the United States and Mexico to choke off the influx of illegal Mexican immigrants. "The Mexican problem," he asserted, arose because Mexican families were "larger than the average American family" and they lived in "unavoidable overcrowding [and have] badly balanced diets."

Pomeroy backed up his claims with the views of other experts, such as Dr. Ernest A. Sweet, a former employee of the U.S. Public Health Service. In trying to show that Mexicans were a danger to the state's citizens, Sweet managed to stereotype two groups in one sentence, claiming, "Mexicans are possessed of an extremely low racial immunity [to TB], which is probably due to their large admixture of Indian blood." There was absolutely no scientific basis for this assertion.

Similar flawed reasoning was used to condemn the Japanese and Filipino peoples. "There is no doubt," the Board of Health proclaimed, that most citizens who died every year from TB "contracted the disease from cases coming here without the means of proper care." The notion that recent, poor arrivals were the problem was then driven home: These "infected strangers, living in dark and ill-ventilated rooms, eating at cheap restaurants and expectorating everywhere, will infect more natives than ten times the number who reside in good homes where care is exercised."

Pomeroy's solution was to urge the state to deport all immigrant people who came from Mexico, Japan, and the Philippines, whether they were in the state legally or not. His request was refused, though not because the state of California wanted to protect the rights of these people. Resistance came from farmers who claimed they wouldn't be able to harvest their crops without thousands of migrant laborers, and from wealthy individuals worried

A U.S. Border Patrol officer stopping cars and trucks at the California-Mexico border in a search for illegal immigrants during the 1930s.

that they wouldn't be able to find decent, affordable maids, cooks, and drivers.

Edythe Tate-Thompson saw her main job as making certain that California citizens always had superior medical care for tuberculosis. This required a great deal of money, and one way to make money available was to deny outsiders access to expensive medical treatment. One of her first acts as director of the Bureau of Tuberculosis was to cancel the construction of the state's first sanatorium, hoping the cancellation would discourage out-of-state people from seeking free treatment. Then she had posters placed in railway stations across the United States and in Mexico warning that "California provides no free care to residents from other states."

These tactics did not stop the waves of sick people seeking a cure in California. The California Board of Health observed that the state had been "deluged at certain seasons with patients, many

A little boy with TB of the spine in a cast on the porch of his family's home in Oklahoma.

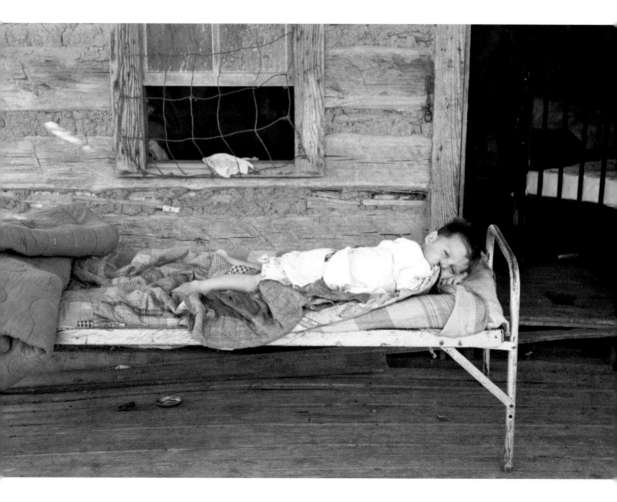

too . . . poor to return home." Tate-Thompson followed this up with a stark warning: "The number of TB cases in Mexican and oriental [sic] aliens which have a high rate of attack overtaxed the facilities available and the financial ability of the commonwealth." The message was clear: Do something about these costly types of people or there would not be enough money to treat "real" citizens.

Pomeroy and Tate-Thompson then joined together in urging immigrants to "voluntarily" go back to their native lands. Both believed firmly that the medical responsibility for a recently arrived tubercular immigrant was that person's place of origin, not the state of California.

They suggested that the best treatment would be found in the patient's native land, administered by loving family members and paid for by the immigrant's government. As an added incentive, California promised to pay for transportation home for any immigrant patient and his or her family. The claim that patients had a choice was disingenuous at best. Because California medical facilities were limited and because minority individuals were often turned away untreated, patients were being told: Stay here and die for lack of treatment, or go home and you might get some sort of medical care.

The drive to force immigrants to leave California escalated in 1930 during the Great Depression. After a request from California lawmakers, the federal government's secretary of labor, William Doak, proposed expelling 400,000 illegal aliens from the state, suggesting that this would help ease unemployment. In a series of well-publicized raids on minority communities, immigration authorities went door-to-door, demanding that residents prove they were in the country legally. Those unable to do so were arrested on the spot and deported.

These raids, as well as pressure from the state, pushed many

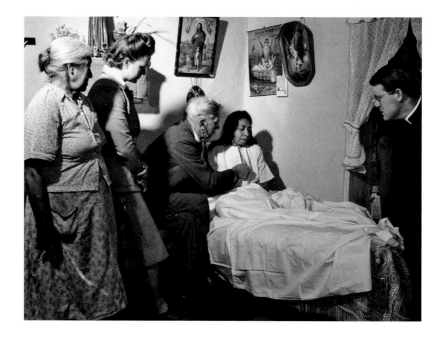

In Questa, New Mexico, the only care this Mexican woman with TB received was occasional home visits by a local doctor.

immigrants to abandon California and head back to their native countries. The first repatriation train left for Mexico on March 23, 1931, with 350 people on board. Within two years nearly 12,800 Mexicans had been shipped south. These trains to Mexico operated for the next ten years, and one major city, Los Angeles, saw its Mexican population decrease by one-third.

Fewer Japanese and Filipinos took the bait. Both groups had strong community organizations that investigated immigration laws and advised their people against leaving. As a result, only a few hundred boarded the transport ships heading across the Pacific Ocean.

While deportation never achieved the reduction in numbers Pomeroy and Tate-Thompson had hoped for, it did succeed in getting thousands of sick immigrants out of California. As one physician who had personally helped deport hundreds of people bluntly put it, "It is a far cheaper method of caring for them than it is to allow them to stay in the County Hospital until they die."

Eventually, reality began to dawn on Pomeroy, Tate-Thompson, and other officials in charge of the state's health care. Whether a person was a citizen or not, whether he or she was present in California legally or not, TB was a growing menace to *everyone*. And it wasn't going away unless all people were given decent medical care.

Over time, more and more poor and immigrant patients received care, though it was often given grudgingly. They were usually housed in clinics attached to hospitals where few doctors were available to oversee treatment. When admitted to a hospital or

Mexican families ready to board the train to leave Los Angeles in 1932.

After much struggle and hard work, these five African American women became nurses at Los Angeles County Hospital in 1940.

sanatorium, a poor TB patient would usually be placed in a separate wing.

Even in the twenty-first century the idea that the battle against disease distinguishes between "us" and "them" persists. In 2005, a nationally televised program began by warning viewers about "illegal aliens putting strain on hospitals." And in 2010 an attempt to extend health care to those who can't afford it was met by stubborn resistance. Some people, it seems, may always be viewed by others as outsiders.

Eight
THE CURE

AFTER announcing he'd found the cause of tuberculosis in 1882, Robert Koch set out to discover a cure. His goal was fairly simple: Find a way to kill *M. tuberculosis* without killing the patient.

As always, Koch worked in a meticulous, deliberate manner. But as the months slipped into years, millions of people with TB clamored for results. Some sent Koch letters begging for his help. There is also evidence that the German government might have pressured him to find a cure quickly. At the time Germany, under the rule of Kaiser Wilhelm and later his grandson Wilhelm II, was pushing to be a world-class power in many fields, including medicine. Koch was employed by the Imperial Health Office and was well aware of this national obsession.

Koch intended to destroy TB once and for all time. The best way to do this, he thought, was to provoke the human body into creating an antibody, a chemical that would kill the rod-shaped bacteria. After eight long years, he thought he had found the answer.

To test his theory, he took pulverized dead TB bacteria from infected guinea pigs and filtered the substance to make it as clean and sterile as possible. Next, he injected it into animals that already had the disease. In a matter of days, they showed some signs of improving.

Instead of testing his results in animals over and over again, Koch decided to move forward and try this experiment on humans. He wasn't certain how the human body would react to the formula. Therefore, even though he didn't have TB, Koch chose to inject himself first. "Three or four hours after the injection," he recalled later, "I felt pains in the limbs, fatigue, inclination to cough, difficulty breathing, all of which speedily increased." This was followed by a "violent fit of shivering" and a rapid rise in temperature

Robert Koch studying slides of an infectious viral disease in his laboratory.

accompanied by "sickness [and] vomiting." After several days these side effects went away.

Instead of taking his immediate and severe reaction to the injection as a warning, Koch viewed it as a positive sign that his formula was fighting bacteria in his system. He decided that he was ready to begin experimentation on individuals with the disease.

The TB patients he inoculated had reactions much like his own. But then something astonishing happened to patients with tuberculosis of the skin: the spots on their faces turned brown, began to shrink, and eventually disappeared. Koch assumed that something similar was happening to patients with TB of the lungs: that the injected matter was attacking the active TB there and the dead material was being spat or vomited out.

The good news was that some patients seemed to be cured by the injection of what was initially called Koch's lymph, later renamed tuberculin. Others had their symptoms relieved for a while, even though they still carried the TB germ. The bad news was that the severe side effects of the injections could last for weeks on end and were accompanied by terrible headaches and general depression.

too BUR kew lin

In the past, Koch would have taken the time to examine these very mixed results carefully. He would have done more testing until he knew for certain whether his formula worked or not. Koch never bothered to do these experiments, and he never explained why. Instead, he chose to announce his findings at the Tenth International Congress of Medicine in 1890. After a detailed explanation of his testing methods and observations, Koch hinted that he had discovered a substance that "in some cases" could protect individuals from tuberculosis and "under certain circumstances" actually cured the patient of disease.

Although Koch tried to be cautious, his words had an immediate and electrifying effect. Koch was so revered for his past discoveries and his careful research methods that his words were immediately interpreted to mean he'd found the long-sought-after cure.

The British medical journal the *Lancet* ran an editorial that proclaimed Koch's announcement "glad tidings of great joy." A British newspaper noted that "the consumptive patients of the Continent have been stampeding for dear life to the capital of Germany," Berlin, Koch's hometown. This was no exaggeration. In the first three months following the announcement, Koch treated between 700 and 800 people with his formula.

Although Koch tried to keep everyone's enthusiasm under control, it was impossible. Colleagues in Germany using the "lymph" began announcing cures for numerous cases of skin tuberculosis, scrofula, and TB of the joint and bone. They also insisted that the inoculation had helped many lung cases. The result was that the

A man receives a shot of Koch's tuberculin while a group of doctors looks on.

German government began manufacturing and selling the formula to doctors around the world.

Trouble began almost immediately when doctors in other countries started using tuberculin to treat their patients. Within weeks, newspaper headlines screamed the news that many patients had suddenly died as a result of the treatments. In a three-month study of 1,010 patients who were given the vaccine, tests of their sputum showed that only 13 were actually cured. Most of these had been diagnosed with a mild form of skin TB. The vast majority of the studied patients saw no improvement at all, and 46 of them died.

On hearing that tuberculin didn't cure most forms of tuberculosis, most patients, fearing the severe side effects, refused the treatment. The failure of Koch's formula was soon followed by an even more troublesome report. Newspapers revealed that Koch was to receive a sizeable amount of money from the German government's worldwide sales of the formula. The international scandal that resulted nearly ruined Koch's reputation. But the extreme passions the incident aroused showed just how hungry the world was for a cure, or at least an effective treatment. And many of the cures attempted were drastic indeed.

In Spain in 1907, Dr. Eduardo Fisac stated without doubt (and with no basis in research), "All workers in lime and plaster of Paris are immune to tuberculosis." He then devised a way to have TB patients inhale finely ground-up particles of lime and gypsum. Not only did his cure not work, it actually made patients' respiratory problems far worse.

Other doctors took the idea of introducing various things directly into the body a step further. These experimenters injected substances—including olive oil, dyes, creosote, copper, gold, and pig-spleen extracts—down patients' throats and into their windpipes. None of these substances helped anyone get better, and many made the patients violently ill.

Each failure seemed to prompt researchers to even greater risk taking. One, a German doctor named Paul Ehrlich, was driven to dangerous lengths after he learned he had tuberculosis. Ehrlich created Compound 606, a mixture of various forms of arsenic that proved to be highly dangerous to make and take. Compound 606 didn't kill TB germs, but one of Ehrlich's assistants discovered that it was a very effective treatment for another disease—syphilis.

Of course, not all TB researchers resorted to such extreme measures. One of the most obsessive and long-term searches for an answer to TB was begun in 1906 by two French scientists, Albert Calmette and Camille Guérin. They took a highly virulent strain of *M. bovis* and began working to create a weakened form of it. Using the inoculation principle developed by Koch, they hoped

Many doctors tried to cure tuberculosis by injecting sufferers with a variety of substances. Here Dr. George Heath injects a patient with his "human serum" sometime between 1910 and 1915.

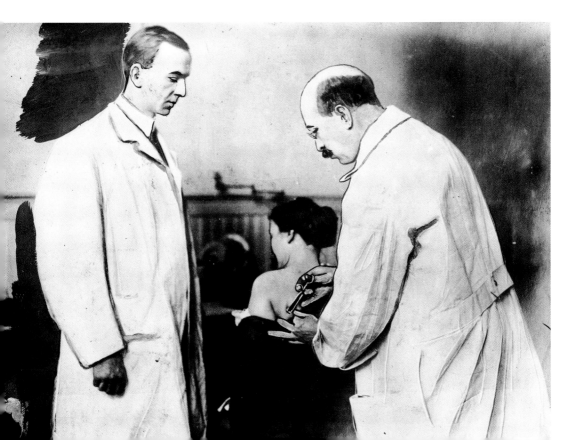

Two of the most relentless researchers for a TB cure were Albert Calmette (left) and Camille Guérin.

that introducing the weakened bacillus in a human would provoke the body to protect itself against invading TB germs.

Year after year Calmette and Guérin struggled to perfect their serum. Even as bombs rained down near their laboratory during World War I, these dedicated medical researchers continued their experiments and testing. Finally, after fifteen years of work, they tested their formula—called Bacilli Calmette-Guérin, or BCG—on a human in 1921. The person chosen was a small baby who seemed likely to contract TB because both his mother and grandmother had the disease. Remarkably, the child not only survived the BCG injection but remained healthy throughout his childhood. The scientists did not track the boy after this, so we do not know if he stayed healthy for the rest of his life.

This test was followed by other tests on humans. The results were decidedly mixed; while many people remained healthy even when surrounded by people with the disease, a goodly number fell victim to TB. Still, in a world hungering for a way to stop tuberculosis, the procedure was deemed a success.

By the late 1920s, hundreds of thousands of people in Europe had been given BCG. Unfortunately doctors and researchers couldn't say with certainty how effective it was in protecting against TB, and still can't today. Numerous clinical studies over

This French poster from World War I reads: "Two Scourges: The Germans and Tuberculosis. The German eagle will be conquered. Tuberculosis must be also." The eagle was a symbol of the German nation. (University of Illinois at Urbana-Champaign.)

Romanian schoolchildren line up to receive their TB vaccinations sometime during the 1940s.

the years have been inconclusive; some suggest that the formula does very little to ward off TB. While the vaccine is still in use outside the United States, many experts, including Dr. Lee B. Reichman, executive director of the New Jersey Medical School Global Tuberculosis Institute, consider it a "widely used but poorly effective vaccine."

All these cures and vaccines—even the most outlandish—were devised by legitimate doctors and scientists. At the same time, other "cures" were developed by out-and-out quacks. Unfortunately, their claims often sounded vaguely medical and real.

Dr. Derk Yonkerman, a horse doctor from southern Michigan, claimed in 1902 that his elixir Tuberculozyne "introduces copper into the blood and the consumption germ cannot live in the presence of copper." He said it had "miraculous healing powers . . . which had been demonstrated not only in early but also in far-advanced and seemingly hopeless cases." This was a bald-faced lie, but there were no laws in place to stop him from making these claims.

Many other syrups and formulas devised by nonprofessionals, often referred to as "patent medicines," vied for the public's attention. Among the most popular were Crimson Cross Fever Powder for the Cure of Consumption, Pastor Felke's Honey Oil, Erben's Healing Inhalation, and Lung Germaine. The last carried a warning label that said, "Initially the germs being torn mercilessly from their lodgements [in the lungs] may induce a feeling of weakness . . . but this is the turning point!" Most of these concoctions consisted of things like pureed vegetables; burnt sugar; olive, almond, or cassia oil; and a fair amount of alcohol. They had absolutely no effect on the disease, although the alcohol did tend to make patients forget about their illness for a while.

Even so, these patent-medicine "cures" proved to be extremely popular. In 1914 alone, the British Post Office recorded handling more than 46 million mail-order packages of patent medicines. Several factors aided their popularity. First, the companies that produced them almost always promised a cure, something all TB patients wanted and were willing to pay for. Second, these elixirs cost only a few dollars a bottle. And the alcohol in their formulas relaxed patients and made them feel good. In general, although they didn't cure TB, patent medicines caused a great deal less physical suffering than many of the doctor-approved cures.

In 1912, while patent medicine sales were booming, the

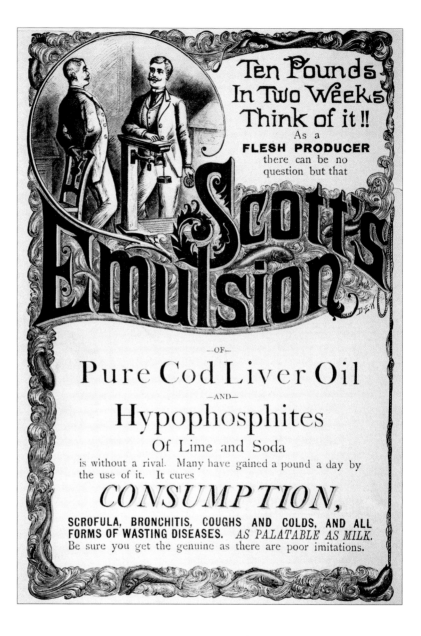

Scott's Emulsion was among the many patent medicines that claimed to cure tuberculosis and "all forms of wasting diseases."

new mo THOR ax

International Congress on Tuberculosis officially endorsed what would become one of the most brutal forms of TB treatment. Known as artificial pneumothorax, it was a surgical procedure that collapsed the infected lung of a TB patient.

The idea had first been put forward in the 1880s by an Italian surgeon named Carlo Forlanini. He reasoned that the sanatorium rest treatment was designed to help patients regain their strength to fight the disease. Why not take the concept a step further? Why not find a way to let the diseased lung rest? Forlanini also speculated that a collapsed lung would keep oxygen from reaching the tuberculosis germs. Since *M. tuberculosis* can't survive without oxygen, he reasoned that in time a collapsed lung would kill the TB.

Collapsing a patient's lung was no easy task. A long hypodermic needle had to be inserted between one lung and the chest wall so that air could be pumped into the space. This resulted in so much air pressure around the lung that it would collapse.

Accidents and complications were all too common with this

A patient undergoing pneumothorax treatment at an English TB clinic.

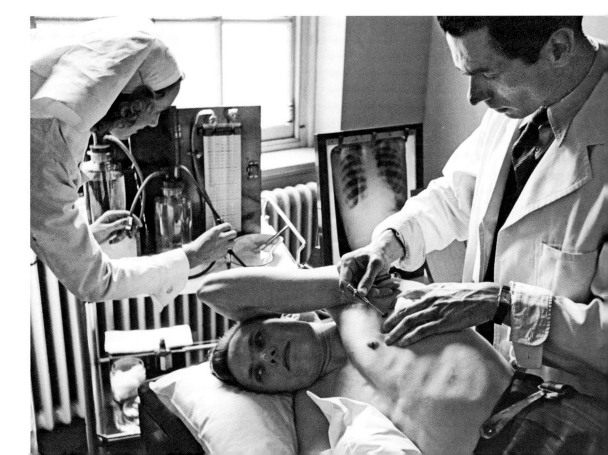

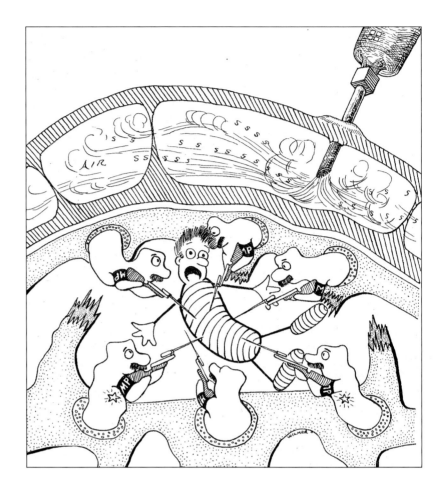

An illustration from a children's book—Huber the Tuber, published in 1942— shows a very distressed TB germ struggling for oxygen as the lung he lives in is slowly collapsed.

radical and tricky operation. Surgeons could only guess where the needle was, which meant they sometimes hit a blood vessel or even punctured the lung itself, both of which could cause internal bleeding. And if an air bubble was accidentally pumped into the bloodstream, it could cause convulsions, blindness, paralysis, or death.

Understandably, not many patients wanted to undergo this operation—that is, until the International Congress on Tuberculosis recommended it. By the 1920s the procedure was fairly common in Europe, and by the 1930s it was being performed in most American sanatoriums. In 1937, for instance, between 60 and 80 percent of all patients in American sanatoriums underwent pneumothorax.

For patients this surgery was not just a complicated, dangerous procedure; it was a terrifying and painful experience. It did, however, offer hope of a cure. Betty MacDonald remembered being taken into the room where the surgery was to be performed. "I was so scared I was practically in a coma," she remembered. "Pneumothorax! Collapse of the lung! I was sure that I would suffocate. . . . I drew air into my lungs in great gulps."

MacDonald made it through her operation and then learned something else disturbing about pneumothorax. The air that had been pumped in would eventually be absorbed into the body, and her lung would begin to inflate again. To keep it collapsed and depriving the TB bacteria of oxygen, she would have to undergo the procedure every two or three weeks for at least three or four years!

Before long, doctors were looking for a way to "improve" on pneumothorax. In one alternative method, oil was injected into the chest instead of air. The theory was that the oil would not be absorbed by the body as quickly as air, so the operation would not have to be repeated so frequently. In another, the lung to be collapsed was cut away from the rib cage, and the resulting space was packed with fat or wax—or, in some cases, Ping-Pong balls.

The most severe and disfiguring procedure was called thoracoplasty. In this surgery, which medical historian Dr. Thomas Dormandy described as "one of the bloodiest operations in the operative canon," the doctor removed from seven to nine of the patient's ribs. With the ribs removed from one side of the body, the chest collapsed, and so did the lung.

Thoracoplasty was so traumatic that between 30 and 40 percent of the patients who underwent it died. Even so, the operation remained a staple treatment throughout the 1930s. Those with advanced TB were willing to take any gamble—even quack medicine or brutal surgery—because there was no other cure.

All of this changed in 1943, however, when a New Jersey farmer arrived at the microbiology laboratory at New Jersey's Rutgers University with a sick chicken in his arms.

Nine

"LIKE A FAIRY-TALE"

IN the autumn of 1943, a New Jersey farmer noticed that several of his chickens were having trouble breathing. When more developed the same problem and one of them died, he worried that something in the dirt where they pecked for food might be causing the illness. He took one of the sick birds over to the local agricultural school at Rutgers University.

The lab there was run by a professor of biochemistry named Selman Waksman. Waksman and two graduate students, Albert Schatz and Elizabeth Bugie, had been studying soil samples for years. They were hoping to find a microorganism that would produce an antibiotic, a chemical substance that would kill harmful bacteria and fungi. The farmer's sick chicken intrigued Waksman. One of Waksman's assistants rubbed a cotton swab inside the bird's throat and gave the swab to Schatz for analysis.

Today antibiotics are familiar to us and frequently used to fight infections. In 1943, however, only one antibiotic, penicillin, was in very limited use. The idea of introducing a potentially toxic substance into a human body was still considered unusual and very dangerous. And with good reason. Almost all past attempts to use chemicals, mineral elements, or parts of animals and humans in this way had resulted in severe and sometimes fatal side effects. However, Waksman and his colleagues were confident that with careful research and testing, they could find a chemical substance safe enough to have a medical benefit.

Schatz had already studied thousands of such microorganisms (and in the end would test more than 10,000). He took the sample from the chicken's throat, went to work, and several weeks later discovered it contained a new form of ground mold he named

Selman Waksman at work in his laboratory.

Streptomyces griseus. The antibiotic drug made from it came to be called streptomycin.

Waksman, Schatz, and Bugie tested streptomycin to see if it would kill bacteria. Not only did it kill a wide variety of harmful bacteria in test animals, it also seemed relatively harmless to the creatures injected with it. This was especially interesting to the research team because the other microorganisms they had isolated that killed bacteria attacked and sometimes killed the host animal as well.

But they hadn't tested streptomycin on tuberculosis. As Albert Schatz recalled, this was because "Dr. Waksman was afraid of tuberculosis." After many attempts, Schatz was able to persuade his boss to allow him to do the test if he moved his laboratory to the basement and never brought TB samples upstairs. Within weeks, the testing had revealed something remarkable. It was clear that streptomycin inhibited the growth of the TB germ. Waksman and his assistants wrote up a paper in 1944 detailing their findings. The paper was published, but no other researchers seemed interested in developing streptomycin into a usable medicine for humans.

The story of streptomycin might have ended there except for a chance visit to Waksman's lab by a veterinary doctor, a pathologist who was studying *M. bovis* in animals at the famous Mayo Clinic in Minnesota. After discussing the chemical with Waksman, Dr. William Hugh Feldman thought that streptomycin sounded promising and took a sample back to his laboratory. There Feldman and his research partner, Dr. H. Corwin Hinshaw, purified the antibiotic and then tested it on guinea pigs infected with TB. Amazingly, within days the guinea pigs began to improve. In fact, several weeks later there was absolutely no trace of TB left in their bodies. Streptomycin not only inhibited the growth of TB but killed it off as well.

Now Feldman and Hinshaw were ready to test the drug on a human. The person they selected was a twenty-one-year-old woman, referred to in research papers only as Patricia P., who was dying of tuberculosis of the lungs. "It was like a fairy-tale," Thomas Dormandy wrote. Within days Patricia P.'s temperature dropped and her coughing lessened. A few months later she was discharged from the hospital, completely cured.

After further successful testing on thirty-four other TB patients, Feldman and Hinshaw issued a very cautious report outlining their results. With the failure of the "Koch's lymph" treatment still fresh in their minds, neither Feldman nor Hinshaw wanted to raise false hopes for the millions of people worldwide suffering from TB.

But word about the cure spread quickly. Doctors from all around the world began asking, sometimes begging, for samples of the drug. Production of streptomycin began in 1949, but even with seven different companies manufacturing the drug, there was not enough to treat all the TB patients in the United States, let alone the world.

Isabel Smith had been a patient at the Trudeau sanatorium since 1928. When the first small samples of streptomycin began arriving in 1946, they went to the most serious cases. Isabel had to watch "with envy the remarkable improvement [the drug] produced in certain select patients." Finally, after a three-year wait, it was Isabel's turn. Over the course of four months she was given streptomycin. An ecstatic Isabel was happy to report, "I breathed not only more easily [and] so far as my wheeze and cough were concerned—well, things were becoming mighty quiet around here."

In April 1949 Isabel's doctor tested her to see if the TB germ was still present in her body. A healthy guinea pig was injected with fluid from her lungs. Whenever the test had been done in the past, the test guinea pig would develop tuberculosis and die within

Selman Waksman (left) standing near a 15,000-gallon fermentation tank for the mass production of streptomycin.

weeks. But this time the doctor "hurried into my room with a smile on his face *that I will never forget.* 'Isa, you're *negative,*' he cried. 'Your guinea pig is hale and hearty.'"

Hundreds of other patients shared Isabel's miraculous experience. On Staten Island, New York City, forty-four patients were given the new "wonder" drug. "All 44 patients with fever," *Time* magazine reported, "had [their] temperature drop to normal within two weeks, most of them within a week, some in a single day. Patients who had picked apathetically at their food became

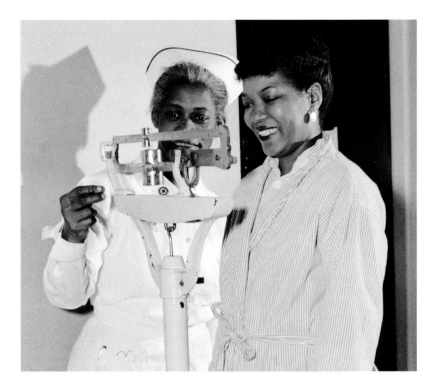

A recovering patient at a New York City sanatorium is happy to discover that she has gained sixty-two pounds in the two months since beginning treatment with streptomycin.

ravenous, they called for third and fourth helpings. . . . Weight gains were amazing. . . . Those who had been bedridden for years were now 'dancing on the wards.'"

An article in the *American Review of Tuberculosis* boldly announced, "[TB] is expected to cease to be a public health problem, and before the end of this century it may become so rare in the United States as to constitute a medical curiosity." Even Selman Waksman gave in to the spirit of victory over a dreaded foe. "Thus, a disease," he wrote, that "was still regarded as the greatest threat to the health and life of man, a threat that hung over the heads of people like the sword of Damocles, has been reduced to the tenth position or even farther back, among killers of human beings."

And it seemed to be so. An ancient killer that had existed for millions of years and had taken the lives of an untold number of people had at last met its match in a tiny bit of ground mold. Tuberculosis would, in time, fade into history and disappear from the face of the earth. Or so people hoped.

Even as the celebration was going on around the world, something alarming was beginning to happen. A number of those who had been "cured" by streptomycin developed symptoms of TB all over again. It appeared that the disease simply wouldn't die.

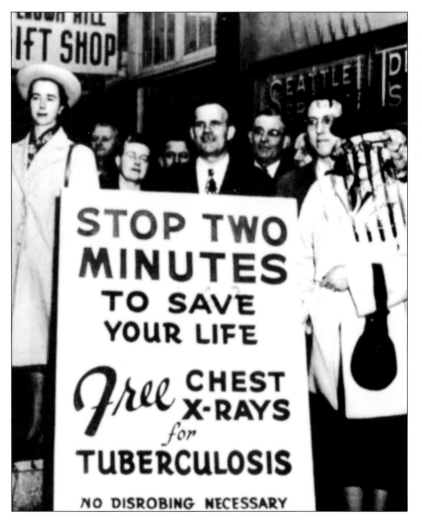

Once streptomycin was available, most TB campaigns suggested that an X-ray and, if necessary, the drug would cure everyone of the disease. Few realized that drug-resistant germs were already a reality.

Ten

SUPERGERMS

IN the records of patient #6, the entry for October 5, 1948, reads: "Temperature normal. No cough or sweats, etc. for eight weeks. Sputa negative." In short, patient #6 seemed to be free of tuberculosis.

Patient #6 had been taking part in a streptomycin study conducted at a hospital in Minnesota. Other entries that followed all gave much the same information as the one for October 5. Everything about patient #6 seemed to be normal. And while it was never stated directly, the implication was that streptomycin had cured the patient of tuberculosis.

However, in early December, another entry was made. It ominously reported that patient #6 has "temp. of 101.3 plus persistent cough. Night sweats back. Sputa positive."

Streptomycin hadn't failed patient #6 in the way that "Koch's lymph" had failed so many in the past. It was very effective at killing the TB germ when the germ was in an active state—that is, when it was multiplying. When the germ multiplied, its waxy exterior split open for a short time, and the germ became vulnerable to the drug. But streptomycin wasn't the "magic bullet" everyone hoped would eliminate the TB bacillus, nor did it leave every patient cured for life.

For one thing, streptomycin seemed to have no effect on dormant (inactive) tuberculosis bacilli. No one is certain why this is so, but it is believed that the dormant TB germ's waxy exterior can protect it from attack. And the human body's own internal defense system can actually help the TB bacillus to survive. When any harmful microbe invades the human body, bone marrow produces billions of a certain kind of white blood cell. These are called macrophages. They are carried by the bloodstream to the site of the invasion, where they surround and kill the germs. During this struggle both good cells and the bad bacteria die, resulting in dead matter called pus.

MACK ro fay jez

But with *M. tuberculosis* the battle sometimes had a different ending. Generally, the macrophages respond to the invasion and engulf the TB bacillus, usually killing it. But sometimes the TB bacteria will break into the macrophages and begin multiplying inside them. Since streptomycin does not kill macrophages, the TB germ might stay safely walled within this protective cover for weeks or even decades. If the bacilli became active after the streptomycin had left the patient's system, the disease could break out of the macrophages and attack human tissue. This meant that patients had to be given injections of the drug for up to eighteen months, and even then there was no guarantee that all the *M. tuberculosis* germs were gone. In addition, repeated streptomycin injections had some unpleasant side effects. The drug sometimes caused depression, muscle aches, and in a few cases temporary deafness.

The side effects were minor compared to another alarming problem: some of the active TB germs began to resist the medicine.

Because most patients began to feel better after just a few days of taking streptomycin, many assumed they were cured and simply stopped taking the drug. What is more, some doctors didn't give patients streptomycin for a long enough period of time. Both situations allowed the strongest germs (the ones that resisted the drug) to survive. The strong bacilli would then begin to multiply, producing millions and millions of supergerms.

Fortunately for those with TB, other antibiotics, such as para-aminosalicylic acid (PAS) and isoniazid, came onto the market soon after streptomycin appeared. While neither of these drugs proved to be perfect by itself, it was found that combining one or both with streptomycin was an effective, permanent cure.

In 1940, 50 percent of all people with active TB could expect to die within five years. By 1950 most were being cured and going on to live normal, healthy lives. But as more and more former tuberculosis sufferers survived, something else started to die: the sanatoriums.

As beds began to empty, the sanatoriums were forced to change. Wings to the large buildings were closed off to save on expenses; some institutions sold off parcels of land to stay in business. And because very few patients were enduring the bloody and brutal thoracoplasty, surgeons began switching specialties, many performing heart operations instead.

Within four years of the introduction of streptomycin, sanatoriums began to close. Many were demolished; a few became ski resorts or tourist hotels. The New York State sanatorium at Ray Brook was converted from a place that housed TB victims to one that housed criminals. In the fall of 1954 a former professional baseball player, Larry Doyle, ate his last meal at the head of a long, empty table, folded his napkin neatly, and strolled out of the dining hall. He had been a patient at the Trudeau Sanatorium since

1942; now he was the very last patient to leave the facility before it shut its doors forever.

A new era had begun. In 1900, when the first truly reliable statistics on the disease were collected, tuberculosis was causing approximately 185 deaths per 100,000 people in the United States. By 1967, the number of deaths per 100,000 had dropped to just 4. New antibiotics (including viomycin, cycloserine, capreomycin, and the rifomycin family of drugs) were being developed that were cheaper than existing ones and very effective. If this trend continued, it seemed likely that tuberculosis, the greatest killer in history, would be eradicated completely.

The seeming conquest of TB resulted in all levels of government cutting back on funding for the study and treatment of the disease. Public health agencies began to lose employees; research facilities closed or shifted their attention to other diseases. In general people

The five-hundred-bed Waverly Hills Sanatorium in Kentucky after it was finally closed in 1961.

began to forget what living in the shadow of tuberculosis was like.

Then, in New York in 1979, the inevitable happened. TB came back, and it came back changed.

Unfortunately, only a handful of doctors noticed that TB was spreading in the city in the 1980s, and no action was taken. Not until 1991, when Dr. Margaret Hamburg was appointed New York City health commissioner, was the alarm sounded. Not only did she document and publicize the rising number of TB cases being treated in local hospitals, she noted that many of these cases were resistant to not one but many of the drug therapies available. Multi-drug-resistant (MDR) tuberculosis had arrived.

But it didn't arrive alone. Another disease called AIDS, caused by a virus known as HIV, had begun infecting people at an alarming rate. HIV caused illness in a very different way than TB did. It attacked an individual's immune system, the part of the body that fights off germs. This meant people with AIDS could then get sick from the kinds of germs our bodies normally fight off, especially the easily transmitted tuberculosis.

Though this new epidemic of TB spread beyond New York City and across the United States, very few people knew about it. Most epidemics brought to the public's attention strike suddenly, downing thousands and thousands of people in a very short time. TB, even the multi-drug-resistant variety, works very, very slowly. At its height between 1989 and 1992, no more than 450 patients in New York City had active MDR-TB at any one time, and the entire epidemic involved no more than 4,000 cases per year.

Yet Dr. Hamburg and other health officials were extremely worried. If they couldn't figure out how to treat this new strain of TB, it would inevitably march on to infect more and more people—the patient's family and friends, neighbors, coworkers, even hospital staff members. In time, the nation would find itself in the middle of a catastrophic TB epidemic equal to the one that gripped the world in the nineteenth and twentieth centuries.

Fortunately, Dr. Hamburg did not have to fight the disease on her own, as Dr. Biggs had at the close of the nineteenth century. Along with the support of the Centers for Disease Control (CDC) in Atlanta as well as the American Lung Association, she was able to get the full support of local, state, and federal governments. Hamburg and her colleagues persuaded New York to increase its funding for TB from $2 million in 1979 to $35 million in 1982. By 1992 New York City was devoting over $100 million annually to the study and treatment of the new form of TB. The bulk of the money went to reestablishing the health-care system that had helped combat TB in the past. Special hospitals were once again set up to deal with the new strain of tuberculosis; additional personnel were hired and trained.

The biggest change came in how drug therapies were administered. Research made it clear that MDR-TB had developed because either patients didn't complete their drug therapy or physicians hadn't administered the drugs correctly. To address the problem, Hamburg turned to an idea introduced by the medical director for the University of Colorado, Dr. John Sbarbaro, in 1979: directly observed therapy (DOT). Treatment was to be administered at public health clinics, at the patient's home or place of work, or at any other convenient location, whether it was a subway station, ferry terminal, or neighborhood bar. This made the process much easier for very poor individuals who might otherwise not seek treatment or have their own doctor.

Everyone involved, from the patient to the manager of the clinic to the supervising physician, was required to sign a contract. In the contract the patient promised to come to all scheduled appointments or to notify the clinic when this wasn't possible. Additional incentives included transportation to the treatment site and food coupons.

For its part, the clinic agreed to make all appointments as brief as possible and to provide medication for free. And finally, the attending physician pledged to provide the most advanced and effective therapy available and to answer any questions the patient might have.

Since completing this course of treatment will cure most people of TB, why wouldn't someone with TB follow through on the drug therapy? One answer came from a medical student named Beth Malasky. Malasky had been a volunteer in the pediatric unit of University Hospital in Newark, New Jersey, and had spent many months playing with a young patient who had multiple-drug-resistant TB. One day Malasky's skin test turned up positive, indicating she had a dormant form of TB.

Rebecca Stevens, a fieldworker in the National Tuberculosis Program at the University of Medicine and Dentistry of New Jersey, reprimands a client who has stopped taking her medicine.

She knew that if her tuberculosis became active, she would have only a fifty-fifty chance of surviving it. Even so, the drug therapy proved to be a burden. "Eight pills a day," she recalled. "They were

very large and hard to get down. I would gag when I tried to take them. The idea of not taking anything and hoping I wouldn't get sick was very appealing. I understood why patients don't comply with treatment."

Directly observed therapy can be delivered in the home, in a park, in a restaurant, or in the workplace. Here people line up at a clinic in Bangladesh.

Malasky completed her full course of drugs and was cured. And so were the majority of TB sufferers during the epidemic. DOT proved to be an efficient way to ensure that treatment was completed as easily as possible for patients. "I never thought we could make as big a difference as we did," Dr. Hamburg commented. "There was an astounding decline in multi-drug-resistant TB cases—91 percent."

Once again, the number of tuberculosis victims dropped, and the epidemic in the United States was stopped. The sad truth, however, was that while the disease had been brought under control in New York, the epidemic continued to rage in other parts of the world. What is more, it would find its way back into the United States again and again.

Eleven
HOT SPOTS

THERE was nothing out of the ordinary about the September 1998 flight from Paris to New York. It seemed completely routine. The 300 passengers waited excitedly in the crowded passenger lounge before boarding the plane. Once they had boarded, there was a half-hour delay on the runway. Finally the plane took off, and seven and a half hours later it landed at JFK Airport in New York.

If asked what they remembered about the flight, most people would probably recall seeing a movie, having a meal, or strolling to and from the restrooms. Few would recall the passenger in seat 30E. He was a young man in his mid-thirties from the eastern European country of Ukraine. A few people sitting closest to him noticed that he coughed a great deal. Only his wife knew that he had active tuberculosis.

Why was he allowed to board the plane? Every year more than 50 million people come to the United States, most of them either as tourists, for work, or to attend school. Only the 660,000 who are seeking permanent immigration status are checked for TB. The rest fly in unexamined and then wander freely through our cities and towns. Another 5 to 7 million are illegal immigrants, often from poorer countries where TB may be a major problem.

As it turned out, the man from Ukraine had been checked for active TB one month before his flight, and the test results had been negative; that is, his TB was dormant. However, his tuberculosis had become active just days before he boarded the plane. Every time this man coughed, he sent into the air millions and millions of TB bacteria that could infect anyone nearby who might inhale them. The rest were sucked into floor air vents and recirculated with the air flow throughout the plane. While some planes are equipped with highly efficient air filters, even they cannot completely clean the air of *M. tuberculosis.*

Three days after landing, this young man felt so weak that he visited a public health clinic in a small town in western Pennsylvania. Despite the fact that TB is very rare in that part of the state, the physician at the clinic was alert enough to suspect that the man had the disease. The doctor immediately called Bill Barry, the senior health advisor of the Division of Tuberculosis Elimination of the Centers for Disease Control.

Barry and the doctor immediately began working hand in hand. The doctor took sputum samples and had them tested: all samples came back positive for TB. The doctor then put the man on a five-drug course of medicines, hoping one or more of them would begin killing the bacteria.

He also sent the sputum samples off to three laboratories to see which drugs would or wouldn't work. Because of TB's very slow rate of reproduction, the first result took over a month to come in: the man's type of tuberculosis was resistant to six of the nine drugs used to treat TB. His medications were changed, and he began what turned out to be sixteen months of treatment.

Getting this patient on the proper medications was an important step, but it was only the first phase of Barry's work. Next he had to find out if any of this man's 299 fellow passengers might have caught TB from him. He began by searching for the 36 people who were sitting closest to the man, as well as the entire flight crew. If it appeared that the disease had spread beyond this group, Barry would have to find all the passengers on the plane.

Locating passengers from an international flight wasn't easy. First, the airline company involved would not release the names or contact information of the flight crew. A spokesperson promised Barry that the flight crew would be notified about the situation, but there is no proof that this was actually done.

Second, many of the passengers were still traveling somewhere in the United States and had left no forwarding addresses. Others could not be traced in their homelands. Still, after three months of dogged detective work and the help of the CDC's Quarantine Station in New York, Barry was able to contact 33 of the 36 people who had been sitting near the young man. Of these, eleven tested positive for the disease, including the man's wife. In addition, two of his relatives, with whom he was staying in the United States, tested positive as well. None of these were active TB cases and all were treated successfully.

All eleven from the plane had come from Ukraine, so it was possible—even probable—that they had contracted the disease there before boarding. They had also sat within a row or two of the man. No one sitting farther away had tested positive. Because of this, Barry and the CDC concluded that the man's MDR-TB had not spread to the other passengers.

This potentially dangerous incident was contained in part by sheer luck, in part by relentless professional follow-up. It exposed some alarming present-day obstacles in the centuries-old fight against tuberculosis. International flights mean that a multi-drug-resistant TB infection can be transported anywhere in the world in a matter of hours. And some areas of the world are producing a high number of MDR-TB cases.

Ukraine is just one of many such places where TB—and especially MDR-TB—is making a frightening comeback. The World Health Organization (WHO) and the International Union Against Tuberculosis and Lung Disease have identified thirty-five "hot spots" around the world where the disease is considered to be of epidemic proportions. In addition to Ukraine, this list includes Argentina, South Africa, countries on the Ivory Coast of Africa (many of which have the highest rates of TB infection in the world), the Dominican Republic, Iran, Russia, and sections of India and China (the latter producing 1.3 million new cases of TB a year, of which 160,000 are MDR-TB).

How did tuberculosis manage to make such a strong comeback? Russia is a prime example. The Russian prison system contains over 1 million individuals. Conditions in the prisons are unusually harsh; prisoners are crowded into small, airless cells and forced to live on meager food rations. Along with an absence of adequate medical attention and medicines, these are ideal conditions for the spread of TB.

Approximately 300,000 people are released from Russian prisons each year. A recent study estimated that nearly 90 percent (270,000) of these people have dormant tuberculosis; the other 30,000 have active tuberculosis, and as many as 12,000 of these have MDR-TB. All these active cases go out into the community and spread the disease to an ever-widening number of people. A recent study estimated that one TB patient "can infect 14 other people in the course of a single bus ride."

Unfortunately, many Russian doctors still insist on treating TB

Russian prisoners in a cramped prison cell in Siberia.

patients in an old-fashioned way, prescribing one drug at a time instead of the carefully formulated cocktail of medicines that the Ukrainian man received. They do this to save money, despite overwhelming evidence that the modern methods are more efficient. And even though 128 countries, along with the World Health Organization, have endorsed DOT as of this writing, Russia has stubbornly refused to sign on to the agreement. Russian doctors are left to prescribe as they please, and patients often go unmonitored.

The situation there was made worse in the 1990s, when the breakup of the Soviet Union caused a serious economic downturn. With money in short supply and budgets shrinking, hospitals couldn't afford to maintain adequate staffing or order new medicines. A wide variety of infectious diseases increased, with the rate of TB infections going up 28 percent. One population expert at

Georgetown University predicted that deaths due to TB would result in a decrease of 10 million in the Russian population by 2015. And if the downward trend isn't stopped, Russia's population could sink from 148 million in 1990 to as low as 80 million by 2050.

Other countries face a host of similar problems, such as political chaos and corruption, economic troubles, social unrest, and a lack of medical experts and medication. These situations make it difficult to contain and deal with the spread of tuberculosis. Already 2 billion people—one-third of the world's population—carry the tuberculosis germ, including at least 15 million people in the United States. Of these, 2 to 3 million will die every year, but not before each infects an estimated ten to twenty other people.

Surprisingly, many people in the world's wealthier countries don't seem alarmed about TB. They reason that the hot spots are in

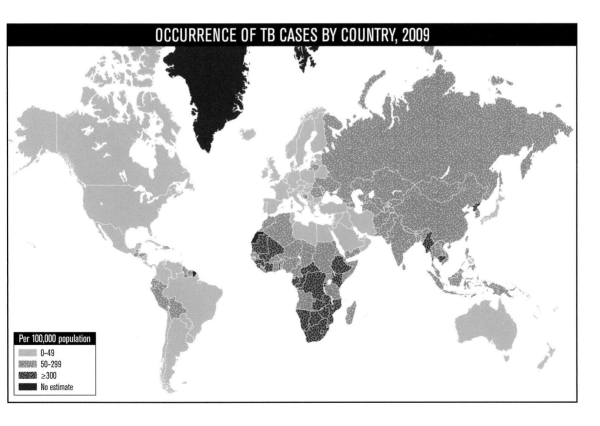

OCCURRENCE OF TB CASES BY COUNTRY, 2009

Per 100,000 population
0–49
50–299
≥300
No estimate

other nations thousands of miles away, so an MDR-TB epidemic isn't likely to reach them. But as we've seen with the Ukrainian man, the epidemic is closer—much closer—than most people realize.

"Our previous hopeful outcome [about TB] is now uncertain," warns Dr. Lee B. Reichman, executive director of the New Jersey Medical School Global Tuberculosis Institute. "Diseases travel with people, and never has it been easier and faster to travel. No place on earth"—and no disease—"is more than 24 hours away from another." And what would happen if our health-care providers failed to react to a new infectious invasion? "Once MDR-TB is unleashed," warns the World Health Organization, "we may never be able to stop it."

All of this is alarming enough, but then *M. tuberculosis* has man-

The jacket of an alarming 2001 book.

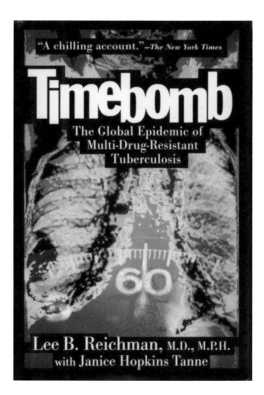

While the campaign to fight drug-resistant TB continues to grow around the world, the message regarding prevention of TB remains much the same. This English-language poster was displayed widely in India.

aged to surprise everyone once again. A new, even more drug-resistant form of the germ has evolved in recent years, one that resists almost all the TB drugs available. This new TB germ is referred to as XDR-TB (extensively drug-resistant TB). Even after two years on as many as six drugs, people who have XDR-TB have only a 50 percent chance of survival.

The situation may seem hopeless, as if humans are in a fight against a very clever enemy we can never defeat. But health-care officials remain optimistic that the worldwide TB epidemic can be stopped.

In the United States, the Centers for Disease Control has established a Tuberculosis Epidemiologic Studies Consortium, whose task is to strengthen and coordinate TB research throughout the country. Their hope is to push forward promising research about

Following the appearance of MDR-TB and XDR-TB, research into new tuberculosis drugs expanded at research laboratories and pharmaceutical companies.

TB, especially in the development of new drugs and detection techniques, and to ensure that health-care providers are carefully trained and equipped to treat the disease. In 2009, for instance, a senior at Rice University named Andrew R. Miller invented a lightweight and inexpensive microscope to detect TB in sputum. His microscope uses flashlight batteries and other easy-to-find materials for only a fraction of the cost of more expensive models.

Meanwhile, the World Health Organization launched its Global Plan to Stop TB in 1998. This is an international effort comprising 186 countries, their health organizations and research facilities, and more than 200 businesses and charitable foundations. One of their programs includes a coordinated effort to treat 50 million TB sufferers worldwide by 2015. The vast majority of these cases are treatable and can be cured with the drugs available taken with the directly observed treatment strategy.

In effect, the effort is a global version of what Hermann Biggs and Margaret Hamburg did for New York City: educate and even alarm people—in the "hot spots" and in wealthier, relatively TB-free countries—about tuberculosis and the threat it poses to everyone. Participants hope to create pressure on governments and other organizations to continue funding research to prevent, diagnose, and treat the disease more effectively.

On another front, a private company in Switzerland with financial support from the National Institutes of Health and the Bill & Melinda Gates Foundation announced a new, automated test for MDR-TB. The test results are available in two hours instead of four to eight weeks and are 98 percent accurate.

Even one of the animal world's least-loved creatures has been brought in to fight TB. In Tanzania the fifteen-pound Gambian pouched rat has been trained to sniff out tuberculosis bacilli. Normally, to test people for the TB germ, sputum is collected, dyed so that only the germ is colored, and then examined under a microscope. Amazingly, the rodent's results are more accurate. In one test, using the microscope identified slightly more than 60 percent of the positive cases, while the rats picked up more than 86 percent!

The tuberculosis germ has been infecting humans for millions of years and baffling caregivers and doctors every step of the way. Every time a new treatment or cure is discovered, this microorganism has evolved, becoming ever more elusive and deadly. There is no reason to believe that this pattern will change. But acceptance of this reality does not signal defeat. Instead, it challenges us to learn from the failures of the past and to combine self-interest with compassion in a unified, continuous global fight. We

Instead of spreading fear, many modern "fight TB" campaigns focus on a hopeful conclusion.

may never be able to say "The End" to the story of tuberculosis, but we can certainly contain the disease to a point at which it is no longer an international threat. That may not be the storybook happy ending we expect, but it should make us all breathe a lot more comfortably.

ACKNOWLEDGMENTS

We would like to thank the following individuals and organizations for their generous help in providing up-to-the-minute information about tuberculosis research and for their valuable direction in shaping the narrative of our text:

Dr. H. Hunter Handsfield, Division of STD Prevention, National Center for HIV/AIDS, Viral Hepatitis, STD, and TB Prevention; Mary Hotaling, formerly director, Historic Saranac Lake; Dr. John Jereb, medical officer, Centers for Disease Control; Mario Raviglione, director, Stop TB Department, World Health Organization; Dr. Lee B. Reichman, executive director of the New Jersey Medical School Global Tuberculosis Institute; and Dr. N. S. Shah, Albert Einstein College of Medicine.

Young TB patients prepare to celebrate the American Lung Association by flying kites with the organization's logo on them.

BIBLIOGRAPHY

We have approached the story of tuberculosis from three distinct perspectives. First, it is the "biography" of an evolving microorganism. Second, it is an account of how the illnesses caused by this tiny invader came to be treated and cured. Finally, it is the social history of the disease, describing how sufferers were viewed and dealt with by the society around them. This broad focus meant gathering information from a great variety of books, articles, and individuals. The written materials we relied on most heavily are listed below.

Abel, Emily K. *Tuberculosis & the Politics of Exclusion: A History of Public Health & Migration to Los Angeles.* New Brunswick, NJ: Rutgers University Press, 2007. A devastating examination of how health officials in Los Angeles instituted exclusionary measures to limit health-care treatment for minorities and the poor, and how they tried to expel certain groups as a cost-cutting measure.

Baker, Robert. *Quiet Killers: The Fall and Rise of Deadly Diseases.* Gloucestershire, UK: Sutton Publishing, 2007. An alarming discussion of how disease germs can mutate and become more lethal faster than new drugs can be developed to fight them.

Bates, Barbara. *Bargaining for Life: A Social History of Tuberculosis, 1876–1938.* Philadelphia: University of Pennsylvania Press, 1992. Using the extensive correspondence of Lawrence F. Flick, the author portrays the lives of TB sufferers and shows how health care differed according to class, race, and gender.

Byrd, W. Michael, and Linda A. Clayton. *An American Health Dilemma.* Vol. 1: *A Medical History of African Americans and the Problem of Race: Beginnings to 1900.* New York: Routledge, 2000. A scholarly examination of how racial prejudice dominated American health care, and how the American Medical Association made the situation worse.

Caldwell, Mark. *The Last Crusade: The War on Consumption 1862–1954.* New York: Atheneum, 1988. A lively history of how the growth of cities facilitated the spread of TB, how the sanatorium movement dominated TB care for decades, and how Selman Waksman and his team discovered streptomycin.

Carmichael, Ann G., and Richard M. Ratzan, eds. *Medicine: A Treasury of Art and Literature.* New York: Beaux Arts Editions, 1991. A fascinating collection of prints, paintings, and photographs, along with numerous essays documenting medical treatment, the development of drugs and medical equipment, and the most notable people in the medical profession from ancient times to the present.

Cockburn, Aidan, Eve Cockburn, and Theodore A. Reyman, eds. *Mummies, Disease & Ancient Cultures.* Cambridge, MA: Cambridge University Press, 1998. A scholarly examination of how scientists search for clues about disease in ancient times by examining the mummified remains of humans.

Daniel, Thomas M. *Captain of Death: The Story of Tuberculosis.* Rochester, NY: University of Rochester Press, 1997. A clear and concise recounting of the past, present, and future of tuberculosis.

Dormandy, Thomas. *The White Death: A History of Tuberculosis.* London: Hambledon Press, 1999. A wide-ranging look at the history of TB with a strong European emphasis.

Duffy, John. *From Humors to Medical Science: A History of American Medicine.* Chicago: University of Illinois Press, 1993. From the early settlers to the mid-twentieth century, this book examines the slow evolution of medical treatment in the United States.

Gallos, Philip L. *Cure Cottages of Saranac Lake: Architecture and History of a Pioneer Health Resort.* Saranac Lake, NY: Historic Saranac Lake, 1985. A photographic history of the many TB cure cottages that still exist in Saranac Lake and a brief account of the growth and development of the cure industry there.

MacDonald, Betty. *The Plague and I.* Philadelphia: J. B. Lippincott, 1948.

A highly readable and often funny account of the author's sanatorium stay.

Majno, Guido. *The Healing Hand: Man and Wound in the Ancient World.* Cambridge: Harvard University Press, 1975. A very detailed examination of written and visual evidence showing how ancient cultures practiced medicine.

Markel, Howard. *When Germs Travel: Six Major Epidemics That Have Invaded America Since 1900 and the Fears They Have Unleashed.* New York: Vintage Books, 2005. Brief histories of six epidemics, including tuberculosis; how the United States responded to each (mainly through limiting immigration of potential disease carriers); and why this approach will not work in today's world of easy international travel.

Nunn, John F. *Ancient Egyptian Medicine.* Norman: University of Oklahoma Press, 1996. This is an awesomely complete volume about medicine and its practitioners in ancient Egypt.

Ott, Katherine. *Fevered Lives: Tuberculosis in American Culture since 1870.* Cambridge: Harvard University Press, 1996. Focuses on the era of the sanatorium cure and how this gentle approach gradually gave way to more and more brutal forms of surgical intervention.

Reichman, Lee B., and Janice Hopkins Tanne. *Timebomb: The Global Epidemic of Multi-Drug-Resistant Tuberculosis.* New York: McGraw-Hill, 2002. An alarming look at how multi-drug-resistant forms of TB develop, how they can be spread, and how we are attempting to track and contain this potential worldwide epidemic.

Rinehart, Victoria E. *Portrait of Healing: Curing in the Woods.* Utica, NY: North Country Books, 2002. A generously illustrated history of Trudeau's Adirondack Cottage Sanatorium.

Rosner, David, ed. *Hives of Sickness: Public Health and Epidemics in New York City.* New Brunswick, NJ: Rutgers University Press, 1995. A series of essays exploring the relationships among housing conditions, the spread of various diseases, and the growth of the public health department.

Rothman, Sheila M. *Living in the Shadow of Death: Tuberculosis and the Social Experience of Illness in American History.* Baltimore: Johns Hopkins University Press, 1995. Covers what living with tuberculosis was like from 1800 to 1940, using many firsthand accounts.

Ryan, Frank. *The Forgotten Plague: How the Battle Against Tuberculosis Was Won—and Lost.* Boston: Little, Brown, 1993. A fast-paced but thorough

history of the dedicated doctors, chemists, and bacteriologists who sought
a cure for TB and a discussion of how the combination of HIV and drug-
resistant TB have created an even more deadly situation.

Sachs, Jessica Snyder. *Good Germs, Bad Germs: Health and Survival in a
Bacterial World.* New York: Hill and Wang, 2007. A thoughtful study
of how misuse of drugs has helped foster drug-resistant germs, plus a
discussion of the "hygiene hypothesis," an argument that links increases in
immune disorders to oversanitation.

Sontag, Susan. *Illness as Metaphor.* New York: Farrar, Straus and Giroux, 1978.
An incisive examination of the "fantasies concocted around cancer, and
around tuberculosis in earlier times," and how such thinking can be unfair
and harmful to sufferers of these diseases.

Starr, Douglas. *Blood: An Epic History of Medicine and Commerce.* New York:
Alfred A. Knopf, 1998. A compact history of blood and how humans
viewed and used it, with thorough discussions of the theory of humors and
the experiments of John-Baptiste Denis.

Taylor, Robert. *Saranac: America's Magic Mountain.* New York: Paragon House
Publishers, 1988. Tells the story of TB in the nineteenth century, Edward
Trudeau's creation of the sanatorium movement, and how Saranac Lake
changed to become a healing center.

Trudeau, Edward Livingston. *An Autobiography.* Garden City, NY:
Doubleday, Page, 1916. The gentle and caring soul of Trudeau is very
evident in his account of his life and career.

Williams, Guy R. *The Age of Agony: The Art of Healing, c. 1700–1800.* Chicago:
Academy Chicago Publishers, 1996. Rich in anecdotes and eyewitness
accounts, this is a cringe-inducing history of eighteenth-century medicine,
which can be summed up with this Rudyard Kipling verse:

> *Wonderful little, when all is said,*
> *Wonderful little our fathers knew*
> *Half of their remedies cured you dead—*
> *Most of their teaching was quite untrue.*

Winslow, C. E. A. *The Life of Hermann M. Biggs.* Philadelphia: Lea and
Febiger, 1929. A well-documented biography of this health-care pioneer.

SOURCE NOTES

Epigraphs

page

vii "The Lord will smite you": Deuteronomy 28:22. The Holy Bible. Revised standard version. New York: Oxford University Press, 1962, p. 250.

"Yet the captain of all these men of death": John Bunyan, *The Life and Death of Mr. Badman*. London: W. Nicholson, 1808, p. 944.

"Tuberculosis—the disease which destroyed": Frank Ryan, *Tuberculosis: The Greatest Story Never Told*. Sheffield, United Kingdom: Swift Publishers, 1992, p. 360.

"No matter how carefully we scour": Baker, p. 17.

THIS IS THE STORY

1 While terms such as *microorganism, bacillus, germ,* and *bacterium* have precise definitions for scientists, they are also commonly used interchangeably to refer to very tiny living organisms. In our text we have used all of these terms to describe the organism that causes tuberculosis.

1: IN THE BEGINNING

4 Of course, tuberculosis was around long before this young male

contracted it. Details on the origins of TB were found in "Research Paper for the Proceedings of the National Academy of Sciences of the United States of America" (referred to as "A new evolutionary scenario for *Mycobacterium tuberculosis complex*"), vol. 99, no. 6 (March 19, 2002), pp. 3684–89. A summary of this paper can be found at www.ncbi.nlm.nih.gov/pubmed/11891304.

The earliest physical evidence of tuberculosis was discovered so recently that information is very limited. We were fortunate to find a detailed account at ScienceDaily: sciencedaily.com/releases/2007/12/071207091852.htm. For additional details see John Noble Wilford, "Signs of TB in Ancient Skull Support Theory on Vitamin D," *New York Times,* Science Times, December 18, 2007, p. F3.

4–5 Descriptions of *M. tuberculosis* were found in Lee Goldman and Dennis Ausiello, eds., *Cecil Medicine,* 23rd ed. (Philadelphia: Saunders Elsevier, 2008), pp. 2298–307; Caldwell, pp. 5–9. Another source of information was the Merck Manuals Online Medical Library.

6–7 The advent of farming and permanent dwelling places occurred between 10700 and 9400 B.C., an era known as the Neolithic Period. A detailed examination of this period can be found in Peter Bellwood, *First Farmers: The Origins of Agricultural Societies* (Malden, MA: Blackwell Publishing, 2005). For more on the spread of TB that occurred at this time, see Reichman, p. 11; Ryan, pp. 4, 6. A quick overview of Neolithic medicine in Great Britain can be found on the BBC website: www.bbc.co.uk/history/programmes/stonehenge/article2.shtml.

7 In addition to the human (*M. tuberculosis*) and bovine (*M. bovis*) forms, there are three other related mycobacteria. The murine version (*M. microti*) infects rodents, such as mice and rats; the avian version (*M. avium*) infects birds; and the piscine version (*M. marinum*) infects watergoing creatures, such as fish and turtles, and is present in many bodies of water, including aquariums. All three have been shown to infect humans, but such infections are extremely rare and have not been included in our discussion. For more information on these, see Beeson, op. cit. p. 259. Also see these websites: www.

ncbi.nlm.nih.gov/pmc/articles/PMC105214/; www.aids-ed.org/
aidsetc?page=cm-522_mac; emedicine.medscape.com/article/223363-
overview.

8 Mummified bodies can tell us a great deal about health issues and early
attempts at healing. Some very good sources of information are
Paul B. Beeson and Walsh McDermott, *Textbook of Medicine,* vol. 1,
12th ed. (Philadelphia: W. B. Saunders, 1967), p. 259; Cockburn, pp.
42–43, 217; Daniel, pp. 9–11; Dormandy, p. 2 note 2; D. Morse, D.
Brothwell, and P. J. Ucko, "Tuberculosis in Ancient Egypt," *American
Review of Respiratory Diseases,* vol. 90, pp. 524–30; Plinio Prioreschi, *A
History of Medicine* (Omaha, NE: Horatius Press, 1975), pp. 257–358;
Reichman, p. 11; Ryan, p. 5.

8–10 Very good discussions of Egyptian healing practices can be found in
Caldwell, p. 10; Carmichael, pp. 29–31; Majno, pp. 69–84, 90–128;
Nunn, pp. 73–74, 87.

9 "A painful finger or toe": Caption translation and information are
from B. Ebbell, trans., *The Papyrus Ebers: The Greatest Egyptian
Medical Document* (Copenhagen: Levin & Munksgaard, 1937),
Formula 618.

10 "an ailment I will treat": From the Edwin Smith Surgical Papyrus as
found in John Merlin Powis Smith, ed., *The American Journal of
Semitic Languages* (Chicago: University of Chicago Press), vol. 38
(1921), p. 322.

10–11 The word *tuberculosis* was first used by English physician Richard
Morton in 1694, but it did not replace *phthisis* immediately. In 1839
J. L. Schönlein, an Austrian professor of medicine, suggested the
word might be more accurate than *phthisis* because tubercles were
always present, though it would take another four decades before
tuberculosis came into general use.

10–13 Other ancient advances in understanding and treating TB can be
located in Caldwell, p. 10; Carmichael, pp. 33–51, 84; Daniel,
pp. 17–21, 69; Dormandy, pp. 2–4; Majno, pp. 141, 337, 339–41,
348–49, 415–17; Reichman, p. 11; Starr, pp. 17–18; Williams,
pp. 3–23.

11 "almost always fatal": Reichman, p. 11.

2: THE KING'S EVIL

14–17 Discussions of the healing touch ceremony can be found in Daniel, pp. 22–27; Dormandy, pp. 4–5; Williams, pp. 170–75.

16 "God . . . grant that these sick persons": T. B. Howell, ed., *A Complete Collection of State Trials and Proceedings for High Treason and Other Crimes and Misdemeanors,* vol. 11 (London: Haward, 1816), p. 1061; Williams, p. 173.

17 It was sometimes hard to tell quack healers from honest ones during this period. An interesting look at medieval medicine can be found in Nigel Kelly, Bob Rees, and Paul Shuter, *Medicine Through Time* (Oxford: Heinemann Educational Publishers, 2002), pp. 48–61.

18 Additional discussions of the contributions made by Paracelsus, Fracastoro, and Morgagni can be located in Carmichael, p. 85; Daniel, pp. 69–71; Dormandy, pp. 5–7.

18–20 For further details on early advances in medical equipment, see Daniel, p. 71; Dormandy, pp. 7–8, 26, 32–39.

19 "the cardiac region": Carmichael, p. 134; Dormandy, p. 34.

20 The theory of vitalism and Denis's disastrous experiments with blood transfusions are discussed in Starr, pp. 3–6, 10–16. Denis was charged with murder but was exonerated after a lengthy and embarrassing trial: Williams, pp. 224–25.

3: "THERE IS A DREAD DISEASE"

23–25 Information about the Industrial Revolution and its effect on population, the growth of cities, and the spread of disease can be found in Caldwell, p. 9; Dormandy, pp. 73–77, 79–82; Donald Kagan, Steven Ozment, and Frank M. Turner, *The Western Heritage,* 8th ed. (Upper Saddle River, NJ: Prentice-Hall, 2004), pp. 529–33, 539–40, 756–58.

24 "Tuberculosis slaughtered the poor": Dormandy, p. 73.

24–25 The effect of the Industrial Revolution on the health of children is compellingly discussed in Susan Campbell Bartoletti, *Kids on Strike!* (Boston: Houghton Mifflin, 1999), pp. 12, 27–28, 84, 93, 112, 135; Russell Freedman, *Kids at Work: Lewis Hine and the Crusade Against Child Labor* (New York: Clarion Books, 1994), pp. 35–38, 49, 54.

25 "stunted in growth": Dormandy, p. 74.

26 "After being one or two months": Dormandy, p. 81.

"Decay and disease are often beautiful": Dormandy, p. 91.

26–27 The surprisingly positive depiction of TB patients in novels, plays, poems, and operas is discussed in detail in Caldwell, pp. 16–20, 22–28; Daniel, pp. 30–34; Dormandy, pp. 85–100, 100–104; Ott, pp. 12–15; Sontag, pp. 3–4, 5, 11–13, 16–17, 18–20, 25–35.

27 "It was the fashion": F. B. Smith, *The Retreat of Tuberculosis, 1850–1950* (London: Croom Helm, 1988), p. 271.

29 "Phthisis is an illness of the lofty and noble parts": Dormandy, p. 93.

"There is a dread disease": Dormandy, p. 92.

There was little new that a doctor could do to treat people with tuberculosis besides bleed them or send them on a long journey in search of a cure. More about this period of doctoring is talked about in Caldwell, pp. 30–34; Daniel, pp. 62–68, 72–73; Dormandy, pp. 117–25; Ott, pp. 6–7, 16–19.

4: INTO THE MOUNTAINS

31 "the reduced atmospheric pressure": From Brehmer's doctoral dissertation, "Tuberculosis Is a Curable Disease," 1853, p. 1.

32 Hermann Brehmer's creation of the sanatorium cure and its remarkable popularity are studied in Caldwell, pp. 11, 67–73, 88, 91, 94, 96, 171; Daniel, pp. 178–79; Dormandy, pp. 147–57; Ott, pp. 49, 147.

33 "It is amazing the amount one can eat": Dormandy, p. 152.

36 "visited only by hunters and fishermen": Trudeau, pp. 77–78.

"poor, sick people in cities": Trudeau, p. 157.

"a little porch so small": Trudeau, p. 170.

36–38 Details about Edward Trudeau and his Adirondack Cottage Sanatorium can be found in Bates, pp. 39, 75; Caldwell, pp. 11–12, 39–52, 72–74, 132–40; Daniel, pp. 180–84; Dormandy, pp. 176–86, 202; Gallos, pp. 2–26; Rinehart, pp. ix–x, 4–5, 7–10, 17–22; Rothman, pp. 201–3; Trudeau, pp. 29–31, 41, 71–73, 77–131, 154–71.

5: "TO COMFORT ALWAYS"

40 "Sanatorium, I knew what that meant": MacDonald, p. 33.

"Crack goes the whip": Robert Louis Stevenson, *A Child's Garden of Verses* (New York: Charles Scribner's Sons, 1889), p. 49.

41 "To cure sometimes": Rinehart, p. 20.

"a depressing place": MacDonald, pp. 38–39.

41–42 The daily routine in a sanatorium varied from place to place, depending on the doctor in charge and how nurses and other personnel interpreted rules and regulations. Good sources for a look into these institutions are Dormandy, pp. 180–86; Rinehart, pp. 34–37, 39–40, 49–81, 83–95; Rothman, pp. 203–5.

42 "cold sponge": Rinehart, p. 76.

43 "with a rule book": Caldwell, p. 117.

"The smallest details": Bates, p. 201; P. J. Kretzschmar, *New York Medical Journal,* vol. 47 (1888), p. 175.

"Patients must not read": MacDonald, p. 53.

"Pretty nearly all TB patients": Caldwell, p. 118.

44 "There's one thing to be said": MacDonald, p. 59.

"We are going to make you well": MacDonald, p. 60.

46 Although Trudeau was many miles from university and medical facilities that had up-to-date equipment, he was a serious researcher. Several authors discuss his work in detail: Dormandy, pp. 179–80; Rinehart, pp. 23–24; Rothman, pp. 198–204; Trudeau, pp. 205–6.

46–47 The use of animals as research test subjects began with the ancient Greeks in 400 B.C. and is still practiced today, with between 50 and 100 million animals being used annually. Vocal and impassioned protests against animal testing go back a long way; Dr. Edmund O'Meara called it "miserable torture" in 1655. Such organizations as People for the Ethical Treatment of Animals (PETA) and the American Society for the Prevention of Cruelty to Animals (ASPCA) continue to protest animal testing. While we care very deeply about this issue, we have chosen not to explore it in our text. The subject is vast and complex and deserves serious and extensive discussion, and we did not want to shift the focus from the story of tuberculosis.

47 "I was 16": Marie Shepitka, "I Shall Return" (manuscript) (Saranac Lake, NY: Saranac Free Library, 1971), p. 1.

"in tears, crying constantly": Marie B. Shay, untitled manuscript (Saranac Lake, NY: Saranac Free Library, 1993), p. 1.

"The cottage may have been normal enough in daylight": Shay, op. cit. p. 2.

48–49 "a shy, scared, sick teen-ager": Shepitka, op. cit. p. 1.

49 "We were told to put nothing on the walls": Shay, op. cit. p. 4.

"cure chairs on unheated porches": Rinehart, p.138.

"If only I had known": Shepitka, op. cit. p. 1.

6: THE CAUSE

51–53 Information about Robert Koch's search to discover the cause of TB and the public reaction to it can be found in Baker, pp. 22, 27; Caldwell, pp. 21–22, 158–62; Daniel, pp. 75–83; Dormandy, pp. 129–37; Rothman, pp. 179–80; Ryan, p. 12.

52 "became emaciated rapidly" and "Under the microscope": Rothman, p. 180.

53 "In the future": Caldwell, p. 160.

54 "bred into trousers": Caldwell, p. 161.

55 "careful observance of hygienic laws": Winslow, p. 40.

56–57 Details about Hermann Biggs and his fight to establish and enforce public health laws in New York come from Caldwell, pp. 177, 186–95, 282–83; Dormandy, pp. 183–84; Rothman, pp. 183, 185, 187–90, 208–9.

57–58 "With every breath": Leon Stein, *Out of the Sweatshop: The Struggle for Industrial Democracy* (New York: Quadrangle/NY Times Book Co., 1977), p. 178.

63 "look to New York": *Boston Medical and Surgical Journal,* 180, no. 21 (January 8, 1914): 66.

63–64 The story of how postal worker Einar Holboell's simple idea to help poor children with TB grew into an international drive to fight the disease is detailed in Daniel, pp. 44–45; Dormandy, pp. 300–302.

7: THE OUTSIDERS

65 "a Poor boy Afflicted With the . . . Lung trouble": Bates, p. 288.

65–66 Details about Robert Freeman's request to be admitted to White Haven Sanatorium and Lawrence Flick's struggle to provide medical treatment to all people are provided in Bates, pp. 12, 14–16, 19, 288.

66 The historical lack of adequate medical care for minority and poor individuals is documented in Abel, pp. 1–4; Byrd, pp. 1, 398, 400, 402–3; Dormandy, pp. 73–84; Ott, pp. 108–10, 120, 122–23; Rosner, pp. 198–99, 200–202, 206, 207.

66–68 The American Medical Association helped unify the medical profession and make it more professional, but it also fostered racial prejudice and left many minority communities without adequate medical care. See Byrd, pp. 375–93, 400–403.

67 "promote the science and art of medicine": *Scientific and Technical Societies of the United States* (Washington, D.C.: National Academy of Sciences, 1968), p. 42.

68 "there is probably no other country": Abraham Flexner, *Medical Education in the United States* (Boston: Merrymount Press, 1960), pp. 3–19.

69 "caused a disproportionate reduction": Harriet A. Washington, "Apology Shines Light on Racial Schism in Medicine," *New York Times,* Science Times, July 29, 2008, p. F5.

70–71 Information about the migration of African Americans to the north and advances in their care can be found in Rosner, pp. 1–9; Isabel Wilkerson, *The Warmth of Other Suns: The Epic Story of America's Great Migration* (New York: Random House, 2010), pp. 8–15.

72 Chasing a cure, a common practice for those with TB, is discussed in Abel, pp. 5–10; Bates, pp. 25–29, 31–34, 35–37; Daniel, pp. 169–70; Dormandy, pp. 113–16, 117–25; Rothman, pp. 45–56.
"A consumptive": Abel, p. 6.

73–78 Details about California's response to the influx of individuals with TB are documented in Abel, pp. 5–38, 61–76, 86–124.

74 "The Mexican problem": Abel, p. 68.

"Mexicans are possessed": Abel, p. 68.

"There is no doubt": Abel, p. 31.

"infected strangers": Abel, p. 31.

76 "California provides": Abel, p. 2.

76–77 "deluged at certain seasons": Abel, p. 30.

77 "The number of TB cases": Abel, p. 91.

78–79 "It is a far cheaper": Abel, p. 36.

79–80 The eventual change of heart by health-care providers is described in Abel, pp. 125–40; Dormandy, pp. 297–312.

81 "illegal aliens putting strain on hospitals" comes from a CNN report by Lou Dobbs on April 8, 2005. The transcript can be found at transcripts.cnn.com/TRANSCRIPTS/0504/08/ldt.01.html.

8: THE CURE

82–83 Koch's determined search for a cure and the disastrous effects of his lymph formula can be found in Caldwell, pp. 163–67, 250–51; Daniel, pp. 113–14, 171–77; Dormandy, pp. 139–44; Ott, pp. 62–63. A concise summary of Koch's life and work can be found at nobelprize.org/nobel_prizes/medicine/laureates/1905/koch.html.

While Koch's tuberculin failed to cure TB, it turned out to be a valuable part of the fight against disease. In 1910 French physician Charles Mantoux introduced the Mantoux screening test. A mild form of tuberculin is injected under the skin, and the area is examined between forty-eight and seventy-two hours later. If the person has been exposed to TB, the skin will swell and turn red as the body mounts an immune response. Improved versions of Mantoux's test are still widely used today.

83–84 "Three or four hours": Caldwell, p. 163.

84 "in some cases" and "under certain circumstances": Caldwell, p. 164.

85 "glad tidings of great joy": Dormandy, p. 140.

"the consumptive patients": Dormandy, p. 140.

86 "All workers": Dormandy, p. 267.

86–87 In the absence of real medical advances in the search for a cure, a startling number of doctors cooked up truly dangerous treatments, some of which are discussed in Dormandy, pp. 265–72.

87–89 The heroic research done by Albert Calmette and Camille Guérin is documented in Caldwell, pp. 261, 278; Daniel, pp. 131–42; Dormandy, pp. 340–49; Reichman, pp. 31–35.

90 "widely used but poorly effective vaccine": Reichman, p. 34.

91 "introduces copper": Dormandy, pp. 273–74.

"Initially the germs": Dormandy, p. 274.

Quack cures, strange elixirs, and patent medicines have always been around and are still with us today. The Hsin Kuang Herbal Store and Clinic claims that its formula consisting of eight herbs ("and possibly others depending on the particular case") has cured 103 out of 108 observed cases of bone and joint tuberculosis, with improvement to the remaining 5. Information about these "cures" can be found in Caldwell, pp. 10, 39, 47, 53, 206–7; Dormandy, pp. 273–83; Ott, pp. 48–52.

92–93 The aggressive, even brutal surgical attempts to halt a patient's tuberculosis are described in Caldwell, pp. 251–57; Daniel, pp. 195–202; Dormandy, pp. 249–63, 352–60.

95 "I was so scared": MacDonald, pp. 150–51.

"one of the bloodiest operations": Dormandy, p. 354.

9: "LIKE A FAIRY-TALE"

97–100 The Waksman-Schatz-Bugie discovery of streptomycin and Feldman-Hinshaw's improvements to and testing of it are detailed in Caldwell, pp. 13, 263–65; Daniel, pp. 204–11; Dormandy, pp. 363–66.

99 "Dr. Waksman was afraid of tuberculosis": Rutgers Oral History Archives: oralhistory.rutgers.edu/Docs/memoirs/schatz_albert/schatz_albert_memoir.html.

100 "It was like a fairy-tale": Dormandy, p. 366.

100–1 "with envy," "I breathed," and "hurried into": Rothman, p. 248.

101–2 "All 44 patients": *Time* magazine article "Medicine: TB—and Hope," March 3, 1952, found at www.time.com/time/magazine/article/0,9171,890255-1,00.html.

102 "[TB] is expected to cease": Rothman, p. 249.

"Thus, a disease": Selman A. Waksman, *My Life with the Microbes* (New York: Simon and Schuster, 1954), p. 279.

Streptomycin brought immediate fame and fortune to Selman Waksman; left behind and forgotten were his assistants. Albert Schatz felt he deserved to be recognized and sued Waksman; the suit was settled out of court for approximately $250,000. Additional information can be found in Daniel, pp. 213–14, 285 note 14; Ryan, pp. 332–39.

10: SUPERGERMS

104   "Temperature normal" and "temp. of 101.3": Emil Boyen, "The Treatment of Tuberculosis with Streptomycin: A Review of 110 Patients," from *Streptomycin and Dihydrostreptomycin,* H. McL. Riggins and H. C. Hinshaw, eds. (New York: National Tuberculosis Association, 1949), p. 107.

104–6   Information on the limitations of streptomycin and the mutation of *M. tuberculosis* can be found in Caldwell, pp. 264–65; Daniel, pp. 146–47, 210–11, 216; Dormandy, pp. 211–13, 371 note 19; Reichman, pp. 13–14, 37–38; Ryan, pp. 326–28, 340–41.

106   The development of PAS and other anti-TB drugs is discussed in detail in Caldwell, pp. 256–57, 265–69; Daniel, pp. 216–18; Dormandy, pp. 366–68; Ryan, pp. 242–77.

106–7   The closing of sanatoriums and the consequences of effective drug treatment can be located in Caldwell, pp. 14–15, 245–47, 269–72; Daniel, pp. 219–20; Dormandy, pp. 378–79; Gallos, p. 163; Reichman, pp. 39–41; Rinehart, p. 149; Rothman, p. 249; Ryan, pp. 390–91.

108   The relationship between drug-resistant forms of TB and HIV is discussed in Reichman, pp. 145–50, 153, 189, 193; Ryan, pp. 397–405.

110–11   "Eight pills a day": Reichman, p. 152.

111   "I never thought": Reichman, p. 153.

11: HOT SPOTS

112–14   The young Ukrainian man's story and the follow-up investigation are described in Reichman, pp. 1–10, 55.

115   The alarming rise in the TB rate in Russia and other countries, plus the international response, is well documented in Reichman, pp. 47–49, 52–55, 73–86, 90, 93–97, 114–20, 128, 190, 191–92, 193, 215–16;

Tina Rosenberg, "Necessary Treatments: Why the Battle Against Tuberculosis Offers New Hope in the War on AIDS," *New York Times Magazine,* September 19, 2004, pp. 26–28.

"can infect": Nicholas D. Kristof, "A Killer Without Borders," *New York Times* editorial pages, December 6, 2006, p. WK11.

118 "Our previous hopeful outcome": Reichman, p. 216.

119 The arrival of extensively drug-resistant TB (XDR-TB) is very recent, and these strains are still being studied. Our information came from articles in the *New York Times* (editorial, science, and international sections):

Altman, Lawrence K. "Doctors Warn of Powerful and Resistant Tuberculosis Strain," August 18, 2006, p. A23.

———. "Drug-Resistant TB in South Africa Draws Attention from U.N.," September 6, 2006, p. A10.

———. "Drug-Resistant TB Rates Soar in Former Soviet Regions," February 27, 2008, p. A6.

———. "Officials Praise New Test That Can Quickly Detect Drug-Resistant TB," July 1, 2010, www.nytimes.com/2008/07/01/health/01tb.html.

———. "Rise of a Deadly TB Reveals a Global System in Crisis," March 20, 2007, pp. F1 and F6.

Bedelu, Martha. "An Old Disease Needs New Cures," March 25, 2005, www.nytimes.com/2005/03/26/opinion/26bedelu.html.

Dugger, Celia W. "South Africa Confines the Ill to Fight Severe TB," March 25, 2008, pp. A1 and A10.

———. "Extreme Tuberculosis," September 14, 2006, www.tballiance.org/newscenter/view-innews.php?id=623.

Kristof, Nicholas D. "A Killer Without Borders," December 7, 2006, p. 144.

McNeil, Donald G. "Drug-Resistant TB Is Still Spreading at Deadly Rates, W.H.O. Reports," March 23, 2010, p. D6.

———. "Technology: For Nations That Lack the Expertise, an Automated System for Detecting TB," April 12, 2010, p. D6.

———. "W.H.O. Reports Rapid Rise in Resistant Tuberculosis Cases," March 16, 2004, p. A7.

Wines, Michael. "Virulent TB in South Africa May Imperil Millions
    Without Quick Action, Experts Warn," January 28, 2007, p. A6.
In addition, the following websites have been very helpful in providing up-to-
date, reliable information and statistics for this chapter:

    www.cdc.gov/tb
    www.gatesfoundation.org/tuberculosis/Pages/default.aspx
    www.umdnj.edu/globaltb/home.htm
    www.who.int/topics/tuberculosis/en

Photographed in 1908, this man is sitting outside his tiny cure cottage in very chilly Ottawa, Illinois.

PICTURE CREDITS

INDEX

Page numbers in **boldface** indicate illustrations.